EARLY LUBBOCK:
A Cultural View

EARLY LUBBOCK:
A Cultural View

By

Paul F. Cutter

EAKIN PRESS ★ Austin, Texas

Contents

Preface

Several fine tomes deal with the early history and development of Lubbock, Texas: George P. Rush's master's thesis (1934) on "The Formative Years of Lubbock, Texas, 1909–1917," Myra Ann Perkins' thesis (1941) on "Pioneer Lubbock, 1891–1909," Mary Ann Ware's thesis (1941) "Forty Years of Music in the Lubbock Public Schools (1900–1940)," and, most important, the outstanding essays assembled under the title *A History of Lubbock* (1962) and edited by Lawrence L. Graves. But none of these presents a comprehensive view of the cultural or artistic pursuits and activities in the community.

Contained herein is a cultural view of Lubbock from its founding in 1891 to the World War I years. It is the story of a pioneer American community's struggle for cultural identity and respectability during its infancy, its first twenty-five years. Those who settled the town were determined that culture would thrive and grow along with agriculture and commerce, and they set about sinking deep roots in the cultural soil.

Entertainment of a cultural sort — dramas, concerts and recitals of music, recitations, lectures — helped lighten the burden of pioneer existence. Relatively isolated as Lubbock was before the advent of the railroad in 1909, cultural entertainment had to be generated almost exclusively from within. After the Santa Fe railway linked Lubbock to the rest of the country, traveling companies of all kinds came to town. Whether with local or visiting talent, the organized events were held in the town's cultural center. In the 1890's, that center was the county courthouse. In the years immediately preceding the town's incorporation in 1909, it was a place known as the Band Hall. Following the incorporation and the railroad's arrival, the brand new Orpheum Opera House became the heart of the cultural scene. We shall investigate the role each played in the cultural development of Lubbock, and in the process discover a great deal about the scope and importance of such activities in the lives of its citizens.

Besides cultural centers, this study is much concerned with local cultural resources: the music teachers, their music classes, the town's budding thespians, the various orchestras, and above all the municipal bands, of which there were five during the period under investigation here. Bands were a source of special pride to communities of the South Plains, valued not only for music but especially for boosterism. Most every West Texas community at the time had a band, for a good band was a symbol of a thriving town. To hear James Dow, editor of *The Lubbock Avalanche*, tell it, the Lubbock Bands played a significant role in the development of the city, one we shall explore carefully. Editor Dow was interested in the cultural growth of his community as well as its physical growth; he understood the interrelatedness of the two. While Dow's efforts were typical of the fourth estate in pioneer communities, where culture was always considered a positive attribute, were it not for his devotion to Lubbock, reflected in part by a continuous stream of newspaper articles pertaining to its cultural activities, much less would be known about Lubbock's early and rich cultural history.

Regarding acknowledgements, I want first and foremost to express my gratitude to Dr. David Murrah and the professional staff of the Texas Tech University Southwest Collection, without whose considerable help and patience this book could not have been written. The Southwest Collection is one of the University's great treasures. I would like to thank all the citizens who consented to be interviewed and who tolerated this writer's incessant questioning. And finally I would like to thank and acknowledge those whose generous contributions made possible this publication:

Dorothy Secrest
Lou Dunn Diekemper
Linda and Howard Hurd
John B. Malouf
Dr. and Mrs. Max Word
Lubbock Radio Paging Service / Stenocall, Inc.
Pierce and Winn, Architects
City of Lubbock
Margaret's
Texas Commerce Bank, Lubbock, Texas
First National Bank @ Lubbock
Plains National Bank
Lubbock National Bank

CHAPTER 1

The Early Years: 1891–1906

How shall culture be defined for the purpose at hand? Not in the broadest, social meaning of all distinctively human activity including achievement in every field, but in the more narrow sense of those artistic activities generally considered cultural, especially music, theater, literature, dance, and the visual arts. The arts are a form of communication that instructs, ennobles, and entertains. The pioneer community placed an especially high value on the last of these; hence, in this study of early Lubbock, those arts that offer a strong blend of culture and entertainment take center stage, especially music, instrumental and vocal, solo and ensemble, and theater, both local and professional.

For the modern-day Lubbockite, it is easy to take cultural activity for granted. Today the arts in Lubbock encompass radio and television, including a classical music radio station and the Public Broadcasting System. Concerts and recitals are presented by the Texas Tech University School of Music, The Lubbock Symphony, visiting musicians, and the community at large. Dramatic organizations in both the University and the community present numerous plays, musicals, and even opera; and dance productions are sponsored by Texas Tech, private instructors, and a civic ballet. The public schools offer instruction and productions in art, music, drama, and dance. The city also boasts nearly thirty movie screens. But Lubbock did not always enjoy culture in so much abundance. From the time of the founding in 1891 to the turn of the century, the community's growth came slowly; setting down cultural roots was a slow, arduous process.

THE FOUNDING OF LUBBOCK, THE 1890'S

After adopting the State Constitution in 1876, the Texas legislature divided the West Texas region into forty-eight counties, many named after signers of the Texas Declaration of Independence. Thus was Lubbock County created and named for Thomas S. Lubbock, a Texas hero and Confederate officer and brother of Francis R. Lubbock, the state's Civil War governor. In early 1890 Lubbock County population numbered only thirty-three, but by the end of that year, the first large wave of settlers had arrived. Land was the chief attraction, fertile land well suited to agricultural development. By the end of 1891, sixteen farms operated in the county, which then had an estimated population of around 175 people.

In early 1891 the present city of Lubbock was established by the merger of two smaller towns, Monterey and "old" Lubbock, settled some months earlier. The merging towns included ninety to one hundred people and seventy buildings — all of which were moved to the new site beginning in January 1891. Initially, Lubbock was rather isolated. The nearest railroad connections were in Amarillo, over 100 miles to the north, and Colorado City, over 100 miles south, while the nearest community of any size in the area, Estacado, numbering about 200 inhabitants, was nearly 20 miles east. Yet, despite the necessity of freighting almost all supplies and merchandise over great distances, and although each journey took several weeks by mule or horse drawn wagons, Lubbock grew and prospered. Thus, by the turn of the century, the town numbered about 300 residents.[1]

Hardships notwithstanding, Lubbock was a pioneer community that found time for the arts among other amusements and whose citizens included talented performers and teachers, particularly in the George M. Hunt, W. N. Green, and J. B. Green families. As isolated as Lubbock was before the advent of the railroad in 1909, it had to generate its cultural entertainment almost exclusively from within. In the words of Smylie C. Wilson, founder of Lubbock's first band, "If we wanted entertainment, we had to make it ourselves."[2] Willie Mae Hawthorne remembered many social diversions, including singing, play parties, quilting parties, picnics, barbecues, and dances.[3] Group singing was probably the main social and musical activity in the early days. The Lubbock *Leader,* on December 3, 1892, reported one of the earliest group singings, held at the George M. Hunt residence. During intermissions, it was noted, Mrs. Frank Wheelock and Miss Myrta Hunt, who "have such sweet voices and sing splendidly together," favored the company with vocal duets. At first musical activities took place mainly in the town's homes and nearby farms and ranches; and throughout the period under investigation, the home remained the privileged place for "private" performances. The newspaper's social page provides abundant testimony: almost every social occasion at home was graced by music. However, after completion of the first county courthouse in August 1892, its court room became the scene of many "public" social and cultural affairs. It hosted numerous home-town concerts of music and dramatic presentations; traveling companies mounted productions there too. Oscar Tubbs, one of the pioneers, recalled big dances in the court room, and how on one occasion the room was made to accommodate the dancers: "one of the upright columns was in the way, so it was removed and put back later."[4] Others remembered that church congregations and various clubs met at the courthouse before other facilities were erected, and that a Literary Society, organized in 1891, met there too. Moreover, an organ was installed for church services and community singing.[5] For public functions, then, the courthouse quickly established itself as the setting of choice, and, practically speaking, its court room was the only auditorium available.

The Literary Society was among the first organized performance groups; its members regularly put on programs of declamations, musical recitals, and even dramas. According to George M. Hunt, teacher, poet, early settler, and patriarch of one of Lubbock's great families: "One winter the members were divided into two classes, and known as the 'Hustlers and Rustlers.' They met alternately, and vied with each other for superiority in rendering their programs . . ."[6]

Local musicians organized several small orchestral ensembles during the early 1890's. Mrs. George Wolffarth (Lottie Hunt) remembered that the first began almost as soon as there was a town; it consisted of two violins, three guitars, and string bass.[7] Another claimed the following personnel:

> Mrs. J. B. Mobley, violin
> C. A. Boston, violin
> Mrs. W. N. Green, string bass
> Claud Green
> Janie Mobley
> Etta Green
> Myrta Hunt
> Lottie Hunt, piano[8]

And Maggie Lee Holden recalled one including:

E. C. Knight, 1st violin
Mark Lowrey, 2nd violin
Claud Green, string bass
W. C. Hawkins, cornet[9]

Although composed primarily of stringed instruments and piano, these were flexible ensembles whose organization depended upon the instruments played by their members. Lubbock's earliest string ensembles were family affairs composed of members of one or more families, the parents teaching the children. Favorite selections included "Over the Waves," "Love's Old Sweet Song," "When You and I Were Young, Maggie," "The Blue Danube," and other popular love songs and ballads of the day.[10] Very likely, these musicians performed at dances, parties, and major festive occasions such as the Fourth of July and Christmas. No doubt they also accompanied the programs of guest speakers, provided entertainment for distinguished visitors and newcomers to town, and performed at political and other rallies. In short, they played at just about any social opportunity that arose.

A typical Fourth of July celebration would include games and contests, a barbecue cooked in the pits in front of the courthouse and usually large enough to feed the entire county, and after dinner a program of entertainment followed by a square dance inside the courthouse. Though no precise accounts exist, the program of entertainment might feature a speaker, a recitation, or a play by the Literary Society, and certainly music — perhaps a few orchestral selections, some solo songs, and community singing. In later times when civic bands were part of the scene, the program would feature selections by the band and by the town's most proficient solo performers, and it often ended with a short, comic play.

One early-day gathering of particular interest was the "Locust Grove Sociable," held on Thursday evening, December 30, 1897, in the courthouse. Although this pre-New Year's Eve party was for the youngsters, it was probably characteristic of the numerous adult parties of the time and is of particular interest because a printed program, reproduced below, is available. The affair included music, games, and, at ten o'clock, supper. Under the heading "Music" are found musical as well as other artistic offerings: guitar solos, a vocal duet, recitations, a declamation, a poetry reading, and a charade. Closing the musical portion of the program were stop-action group poses called tableaux, and, presumably, non-musical specialty acts. The menu for the supper appears as delectable as that for the music!

PROGRAMME

of the

LOCUST GROVE SOCIABLE

————————

Thursday Evening, December 30th, 1897

————————

MUSIC

GAMES: Chess, Crokinole, Table Croquet, Dominoes, Authors, etc.

Supper at 10 o'clock

MUSIC

Recitation   Miss Blanche Taylor

Charade

Vocal Duett   Misses Nora and Myrta Hunt

Poem, "The Occasion,"   Winford Hunt

Guitar Solo   Miss Lottie Hunt

Declamation   Master Clifford Hunt

Guitar Solo   John F. Raley

Recitation   Miss Lottie Hunt

Tableaux

Specialties

MENU

MEAT.

Salmagundi with Spanish Sauce

Fricased Tripe   Bubble and Squeak

Spider Legs Pickled

PIE.

Pigeon Pie

Chess Pie   Pot Pie

CAKE.

Phoebe's Poverty Cake

Macroons   Kisses

DESSERT.

Batter Pudding

Batchelor Custard   Snow Balls

Finally, the early settlers also took kindly to teachers of the arts, especially music, for they wanted their children to experience first-hand the cultural graces. Among the first music teachers were Mrs. Henry Crump, Mrs. Lee Auten, and Dora Mobley; Lubbock also had two elocution teachers in the early 1890's, Irene Shannon and Mrs. Lou Stubbs.[11] One can presume that the students regularly exhibited their talents in recitals, probably presented in the courthouse, and became a contributing element to the cultural life of the community.

THE TURN OF THE CENTURY: 1900–1906

At the turn of the century the entertainment and cultural activities were still largely home-made, but that began to change. Changing also was the population, which swelled from a county-wide total of 293 in 1900 to a city-wide 800 in 1905.[12] By 1905 the town enjoyed the services of two professional music teachers, T. D. Mullins and Lula Campbell. Traveling music and drama companies also began to find Lubbock large enough to warrant a stop on the itinerary, and local talent increased in quantity and quality with each passing year.

"Professor" T. D. Mullins, whose title was commonly given to male music teachers irrespective of degrees or college affiliation, came to Lubbock in 1905 to teach for the summer. The *Avalanche* editor J. J. Dillard, impressed by Mullins and motivated by the community's need for his knowledge and professionalism, hardly let an issue of the newspaper go by without some reference to his activities. Thus, the first notice informed the reader:

> Prof. T. D. Mullins, a first-class vocal music teacher, was in the city Sunday [July 9] and led a class in singing at the court house Sunday afternoon. A large crowd was in attendance and everybody was well pleased with the work.
>
> An effort is now being made to secure a class for the professor, and we are glad that considerable interest is being manifested.[13]

Mullins then took out the following mildly amusing advertisement that ran continuously until his departure in November:

Prof. T. D. Mullins
Vocal and Instrumental Music taught on short notice,
anywhere, at Reasonable Terms.
———————
Present Address: Lubbock, Texas[14]

Dillard later wrote that the "music school [is] progressing nicely. There has been an enrollment of thirty-four pupils, and we hear highest praises of the work. An effort will be made to get the professor to teach another term when the present one closes."[15] Indeed, Mullins did teach two short terms: July 19 to August 8 and August 14 to September 8, on which date his pupils were heard in recital. In October, he made plans to travel east for the winter, but promised to return in June 1906 for another summer school.[16] We do not know if he did; we do know, however, that he did not return after 1907. Mullins was part of the cadre of itinerant music teachers who each summer came into rural communities, where there often was no resident music teacher, to give classes, mainly in singing. For Mullins it provided summer employment; for the pupils, their only exposure to a professional music teacher.

When Miss Lula Campbell decided to make Lubbock her permanent address is also unknown, but by fall 1905 she was firmly established as Lubbock's first resident, professional music educator, as well as the principal musical force in the community. After assembling a music class, one of her first efforts was to form a choral organization known as the "Union Choir," which numbered fifteen singers and met every Tuesday evening alternating between the Methodist and Baptist churches.[17] Later, she undertook a grand concert for the benefit of the Methodist Church. The event was described as follows:

> On the 29th of November, Miss Lula Campbell of this city entertained a large number of people at the court house with an old time singing school concert. Her music school, assisted by others, entertained the audience for more than two hours with singing, recitations and instrumental music. Miss Campbell possesses great talent as an instructor, and displays wonderful ability in carrying out a program.[18]

Recitals of her music class coupled with charitable efforts in behalf of needy organizations were frequent affairs for the civic-minded Miss Campbell, about whom more will be said later.

Sunday church services were a major setting for musical performances. One could regularly hear Lula Campbell's choir and others. Civic leader Smylie Wilson took a leading role in directing small ensembles at his church: duets, trios, and quartets. In addition to his religious musical activities, Wilson was also busy founding Lubbock's first municipal band in late 1904 or early 1905.

During the summer of 1905, three itinerant companies found their way to Lubbock, remarkable considering the arduous journey: the nearest railroad connection was still about 100 miles away (in Canyon). Professor Thorp's Jubilee Singers presented a "very interesting" concert in the courthouse on August 9. The *Avalanche* judged the professor a fine violinist and his daughter a splendid vocalist, but saved its greatest applause for Mrs. Thorp, a blind organist, "who deserves the praise of all." A big tent show, featuring songs and black-face comedy, entertained on September 2; and Karmont Brothers put on a play, entitled "A Trip Thru Hell," at the courthouse on September 6.[19]

The courthouse was again the scene, on New Year's Day 1906, for a play entitled "Ye Deestrict Skewl" mounted by local talent. Admission was twenty-five cents for adults, fifteen cents for children, and receipts totalled $51.35. A picture emerges of people hanging from the proverbial rafters! If half the proceeds came from adults and half from children, approximately 270 persons or about one third of the population would have been in attendance — a fascinating commentary on the young town's thirst for dramatic entertainment.[20] No wonder, a few days earlier, Editor Dillard, acknowledging Lubbock's recent growth, wrote: "A few years ago either of the [two] church buildings would have seated all the people in the county. Now the town's population can fill the courthouse and both churches to overflowing."[21]

On the whole, the cultural climate of Lubbock by 1905 was most healthy. Meeting the social and cultural needs of the inhabitants were local talent — the band, the choirs, various smaller ensembles, solo recitalists, and literary and dramatic groups — as well as an occasional traveling company; and the needs of the children were attended to by professional music teachers.

The front page of the newspaper's initial issue for 1906 sounded a strong note of optimism for the coming year. Unfortunately, no further papers are available until August 2, 1907. By then the courthouse was no longer the social and cultural center of town; growth had necessitated a larger public facility. The story now shifts to a place known as the "Band Hall."

CHAPTER 2

Lubbock's Cultural Centers, Part I: The Band Hall *

Smylie Wilson's words, "If we wanted entertainment, we had to make it ourselves," still described Lubbock culture between 1907 and 1909.[1] The place where the entertainment was made during those years was known as the Band Hall. Lubbock's first two-story building, at the northeast corner of Broadway and Avenue J, was owned by businessman S. A. Richmond. He and his son-in-law W. Oscar Tubbs operated a furniture store on the ground floor, while the entire upper floor, the Band Hall, served as the town's community center.

THE BUILDING

It is a reasonable speculation that the structure was built especially to accommodate the Lubbock band, but the band was only one of several musical organizations to perform there. The hall was also used for traveling shows, lodge meetings, town hall meetings, guest speakers, and home-town plays.[2]

The precise date of construction of the building is unknown. In an informative article on early-day entertainment in Lubbock, Mary Howell suggested 1905.[3] Smylie Wilson thought "some time after 1905,"[4] while W. Oscar Tubbs of the Richmond & Tubbs Furniture establishment said "1906 — possibly 1905."[5] Construction was certainly completed before July 4, 1907, when a dated picture of the building was taken (see Chapter 4).

Several photographs of the building are known, including the two presented here: Plate 1 of the building itself, and Plate 2 showing it in re-

Plate 1. The Band Hall, circa. 1907.
— Photo courtesy Southwest Collection, Texas Tech
University, Lubbock, Texas

Plate 2. West side of town square, circa. 1907. The Band Hall is the long, two-story building in the upper left.

— Photo courtesy Southwest Collection, Texas Tech University, Lubbock, Texas

lation to the west side of the courthouse square. Entrance to the Band Hall was via an outside staircase at the southwest corner of the building (see Plate 1). The doorway was at the south end of the hall; the stage, Lubbock's first, was probably at the north end. Inside also were dressing rooms, places to store props and scenery, and benches for seating.[6] Seating capacity was around 300.[7]

The building had metal siding, which, several pioneers recalled, rattled so loudly when the wind blew that it was occasionally all but impossible to hear the music! The hall was illuminated by kerosene and acetylene lights[8] — Lubbock did not yet enjoy electric lighting — and, according to *The Avalanche*, it is "the nicest hall on the South Plains . . . [It] is well ventilated and lighted [and] has a handsome stage curtain which is covered with advertisements of the most progressive businessmen of town . . ."[9]

On the whole, a picture emerges of a rather attractive, if on occasion somewhat noisy, multi-purpose hall that could hold nearly half the town's population (the courthouse was the only other such building) and that, because of its stage, saw considerable use by musicians, thespians, and others in the community who found the Band Hall more functional and appropriate for their needs than the courthouse.

EVENTS AND PERFORMANCES

The presence of a hall dedicated to the performing arts, among other things, no doubt stimulated a greater quantity and quality of cultural and entertainment activities in Lubbock. Appendix A lists all known events held in the Band Hall. Even a small part of the list, such as the last five months of 1907, shows that Lubbockites regularly enjoyed the circus, movies, plays and, above all, concerts of music. Quite remarkable is the variety and sheer number of performances taking place at such an early date in the town's history (the population numbered only about 1,000) and in the span of only five months. Moreover, except for the circus (and the moving pictures), all the talent was local, confirming Smylie Wilson's assertion about home-grown entertainment. Isolation forced the inhabitants to provide for their own cultural welfare, and it would appear that they embraced the task with relish.

Indeed, while the entire list of events and performances in the Appendix shows an occasional traveling company or lecturer, it makes clear that at the center of Lubbock's cultural life during the time were the town's own artists. Music teachers Nancy Patterson, Lula Campbell, and Philip E. Baer frequently directed their students in recital, and Hattie

McGee and Willie Cowan, two young ladies of the community active in music making, took the stage often as well. The local thespians mounted their own productions. And at the head of the list was the Lubbock 1906 Band.

According to Smylie Wilson, Lubbock's first band was formed in late 1904 or early 1905;[10] however, it lasted only a few months, disbanding well before construction of the Band Hall. Lubbock's second, called the Lubbock 1906 Band, made the Band Hall its home, renting the facility for its rehearsals and concerts. The achievements of the Lubbock 1906 Band will be discussed in detail in Chapter 4. Suffice it to say here that, in addition to rehearsing in the hall at least one night a week, the band, from August 10, 1907, through February 22, 1908, gave six concerts there — on average, just short of one each month. The concerts were immensely popular, often filling the hall to capacity. Moreover, the band was a cultural magnet, attracting the town's most talented citizens to its stage. As a result, each concert tended to be an undertaking of sizable dimension, an expression of genuine community effort.

All in all, band concerts played a singularly significant role in Lubbock's cultural life; and a deep sense of community loss must have accompanied their end, sometime after February 1908. However, it was by no means the end of music in the community. While the band could indeed lay claim to being the centerpiece, Lubbock's cultural table was quite large. The Band Hall continued to enjoy active use, most notably by the town's music teachers, but also for other musical and non-musical events.

Charitable events frequently brought the town's musicians together in concert, as on Thanksgiving Day 1907, for a benefit for the Lubbock Cemetery (Figure 1). Ross Edwards, a fiddler, recalled that he played for a dance in the Band Hall one night shortly after he arrived in town in 1907.[11] Virginia Richmond Tubbs, daughter of S. A. Richmond, who owned the building housing the Band Hall, remembered that Philip Baer used to teach in the Band Hall.[12] Miss Effie Kelley, another music teacher, moved to the city in August 1907 and promptly gave a recital in the Band Hall; the next month, however, she left for Oklahoma to attend her sick mother and apparently never returned.[13] A local theater group called the Hawthorne Dramatic Club made its debut in the Band Hall on April 7, 1908.[14] Other plays by other local groups were enacted at the Band Hall,[15] and traveling players appeared occasionally as well.[16]

The Band Hall was also home to many other activities. The local chapter of the International Order of Odd Fellows used it for lodge meetings and banquets.[17] Moving pictures were shown on occasion,[18] and it

Cemetery Association Program

The following program will be rendered at the Band Hall on the evening of our National Thanksgiving Day, November 28th, 1907, under the direction of the Cemetery Association. We are making a strenuous effort to add some much needed improvements to our cemetery. The first requisite being a fence. The proceeds of this entertainment will be thus used. We know that all will be interested in protecting the last resting place of our loved ones, hence we feel confident of a crowded house.

Instrumental Music - - "Little Florence Waltz"
Mrs. Norton, Messrs. Wilson and Norton.

Song - - - - "I'm Looking For My Papa"
Eva Wheelock, Bertha Bullock, Jewel Burrus, Mary Dixon, Winnie Clayton and Gracie Brown.

Reading - - - - - "Burial of Moses"
Mrs. Beatty.

Song - - - - - "Very Little Tots"
Freda Boyd, Yancy Lee, Fern Wheelock, Bernice Wolffarth and Opal Ellis.

Reading - - - - - Miss Bessie Jarrott

Song - - "When My Ship Comes Over The Sea"
Mesdames Wheelock and Boyd and Messrs. Norton and Wilson.

Scarf Drill - Misses Griffin, Ellis, Dale, Patterson and Tubbs.

Instrumental Music - Mrs. Norton, Messrs. Wilson and Norton.

"Jolly Little Cupids" - - - - By six little boys.

Vocal Quartette - - "Come Where the Lillies Bloom"
Mesdames Wheelock and Boyd and Messrs. Wilson and Norton.

Recitation - - - "When Company Comes"
Luree Peoples.

Instrumental Solo - - - - Miss Patterson

Reading - - - "The First Thanksgiving"
Mrs. Stubbs

Chorus - - - "Come to the Gay Feast of Song"
Choral Club

Reading - - - "Sally Ann's Experience"
Miss Dezzie Johnson

Song - - - "Moonlight Will Come Again"
Mesdames Wheelock and Boyd and Messrs. Wilson and Norton.

Mesdames B. Boyd, F. E. Wheelock, Mrs. J. T. Bullock
Committee on Program.

Figure 1. Cemetery Association Concert.
— *The Avalanche*, November 22, 1907, p. 7.

even functioned in a religious capacity, providing a platform for traveling preachers.[19]

The sum of all the above activity leads to an unmistakable conclusion: from early 1907 (if not before), the very pulse of the city's life beat daily at the Band Hall. It was the social and cultural heart of the city.

THE PASSING OF THE BAND HALL

The central position of the Band Hall, as well as the era in Lubbock's history of which it was a part, passed in 1909 as the Santa Fe Railroad was extended from Plainview to Lubbock. The railroad would transform the town into a small city, and, flush with the realization that geographical isolation was at an end and that tremendous growth lay just ahead, the citizens incorporated the town in the spring, at almost the very time work was begun on the railroad connection. That work was progressing at full steam by May; tracks reached Lubbock in September; the first work train arrived on September 25; and the first passenger train on October 25. Seymour Connor recaptured the excitement of that moment with these words:

> Naturally, a mammoth celebration was staged. Many people went to Plainview to ride the first train into Lubbock. The newspaper issued a special edition to commemorate the event, and the town's burgeoning optimism knew no bounds. Real estate men advertised wildly-advancing land prices and settlers were urged to converge on Lubbock from all corners of the land to take advantage of the prosperity that was to come.[20]

The Federal Census of 1910 put the city's population at 1938, up considerably from October 1908, when the paper boasted that Lubbock had about 1,000 inhabitants.[21] One inevitable casualty of the explosive growth was the Band Hall. The city needed a larger place for civic and business meetings, social gatherings, and cultural activities. And so, in April 1909, construction commenced on a larger facility, which came to be known as the Orpheum Theatre or more simply the Opera House.

On the tracks of the railroad passed the pioneer era in Lubbock's history, and with the coming of the Opera House went the passing of the Band Hall. One served the pioneer town, a symbol of the past; the other served the newly incorporated City of Lubbock, a harbinger of the future.

CHAPTER 3

Lubbock's Cultural Centers, Part II: The Opera House

America's expanding railway system in the second half of the nineteenth century made possible the wide success of the traveling repertory troupe. The troupes reached their zenith between 1890 and 1920, bringing plays and specialty acts to the opera houses of small towns throughout the country.[1]

OPERA HOUSES AND TRAVELING COMPANIES IN AMERICA

"Opera house" was a euphemism for theater. The latter term carried the wrong connotations; the former, the right ones. The "theater," with its traditional taint of immorality, was a place that disturbed those with conservative religious views, especially in rural America; so plays were given instead in more respectable places such as the Opera House, Town Hall, Music Hall, or Concert Hall.[2] Lubbock had a Band Hall in 1907 and, beginning in 1909, an Opera House. So too did dozens of other Texas communities serviced by the railroad.

Opera house managers could offer their patrons a great variety of entertainments: opera, musical comedy, concerts by professional bands, singers, and instrumentalists, minstrel shows, wild west shows, vaudeville, one-night-stand dramatic companies, and repertory companies that came to town usually for a week, presenting a different play each night.[3] Lubbock's Opera House managers presented most such entertainments, but repertory companies took the lion's share of the bookings (See Appendix B).

What kind of theater most appealed to rural America? Just as the popular audience for music preferred patriotic songs and marches to symphonies and sonatas, so its counterpart for drama preferred a diet of frothy fare and melodrama to Shakespeare, Sheridan and Shaw. Rural audiences were often unwilling to support drama of high artistic merit, but were eager to embrace grass roots theater, "a common man's culture."[4] The plays accepted and applauded represented not great literature but homely tastes, desires and values. Most had a moral or message, and the main themes were nationalism, patriotism, sentimentality, traditional values, and the virtues of the common folk.[5] Hence, comedy, musical comedy, and Shakespearean drama were to play only subsidiary roles, while the leading part went to melodrama, which proved the most enduring formula for American popular theater and which dominated the rural stage during the late 1800's and early 1900's. Robert Toll, in his book *On With The Show*, suggests:

> Because melodrama exalted the traditional values to which people desperately clung in the face of fundamental change, audiences credited melodrama with being more real than reality, a higher truth that transcended everyday experience. An ideal statement of the way life ought to be, melodrama made evil and corruption easy to identify and solutions easy to find; it made heroes of common, simple people; and it made virtue and the virtuous triumph . . . Melodrama served perhaps an even more important, certainly more concrete and immediate function for audience members by providing an outlet for their feelings and emotions — a chance to scream, to laugh, to gasp, and to cry. It was . . . a celebration of the traditional American way of life.[6]

A study of the fifty-seven plays known by title to have been presented in Lubbock from 1909 to 1915 (see Appendix B) is beyond the scope of this book, but without doubt melodrama took center stage.

The troupers themselves usually carried a week's worth of plays in their repertory as well as sufficient musical, vaudeville, or other specialty numbers to entertain the audience between acts. While some troupes specialized in one-night stands, for most it made more economic sense to remain several days to a week at each stop. Besides, traveling was scarcely comfortable at the turn of the century, even by railroad; staying in each town a week gave the troupe time to rest and recover.[7]

The players normally came to town between September and May, *i.e.*, during the "winter" theater season. In days before air-conditioning, indoor theater circuits of necessity operated during the winter season.

Outdoor entertainment was available during summer, courtesy of Chautauquas and other tent shows, but mainly at cool suburban or resort locations, by a lake or the sea.

THE BUILDING

By early 1909 it seemed that everyone in Lubbock had come down with growth fever, courtesy of the Santa Fe Railroad. The certainty of the connection from Plainview and the prospect of other lines through the city already had people talking about Lubbock as the hub of the Plains. The editor of the newspaper proudly boasted the town's achievements and boosted its prospects in nearly every issue, and real estate promoters were having a field day. Advertisements like the following were typical:[8]

Dillard–Marshall Land Company

The Santa Fe Branch will be completed from Plainview to Lubbock within a few months. That will carry prices above what they are at present . . . The completion of the Santa Fe Branch will double prices of land. The completion of the Santa Fe Cut-off will double these prices. The completion of the Altus will double that again. With these three roads, and with others practically assured, Lubbock is certain to make the biggest town in all the Plains Country . . .

Similarly, a *Lubbock Avalanche* editorial proclaimed:

The slightest doubt has vanished from the minds of this town that this place will be the city of the plains in a very few years. She has advantage of nearly every town on the plains, and the railroads are coming this way in bunches, and there is certainly going to be something doing for Lubbock from this day on . . .

It was in this optimistic atmosphere that Lubbock's opera house was built. Two businessmen, Charles Reppert and Ralph Erskine (Jink or Jinks) Penney, saw the potential of such an enterprise to a town whose growth the railroad would assure. Realizing that Lubbock would soon be hosting traveling troupes in great numbers, and anticipating that an opera house would be viewed by a rapidly growing community as a great cultural asset, they undertook construction of the facility. The initial notices of the venture appeared in the April 1 and April 8, 1909 newspapers:

[1.] The amusement building being erected by Messrs. Penney & Reppert, will be completed in a few days. This building will be thirty by ninety feet with a fifteen foot stage fifty feet wide, and will be especially designed and provided for high class entertainments of different kinds. Among other things they have secured a very elaborate and up-to-date selection of moving pictures. These people have donated the use of their building to the commercial club for the meeting here on the 21st. The town has long felt the need of a more commodious place for public gatherings, and this amusement building which will be known as the Orpheum Theatre.

[2.] The amusement building being erected by Messrs. Penney & Reppert . . . will be ninety by forty feet, and will have ample seating capacity, and is a much more commodious place for a public gathering . . . than either the present opera house or the courthouse, owing to the fact that it will accommodate a much larger number of people.

While there seems to have been some discrepancy over the actual dimensions — 30′ X 90′ or 40′ X 90′ — there was none whatever on the relatively greater size of the new opera house compared to "the present opera house" (the Band Hall): 2,700 square feet or 3,600 square feet versus about 1,650 square feet. Furthermore, its larger stage would be more attractive to the many stock and vaudeville companies that were now to pass through Lubbock on the railway.

Unfortunately, no photographs of the Opera House are available. Its location was on the site of the downtown Hemphill-Wells/Hester's building. The outside must have been somewhat non-descript; Lubbock citizens seem to remember more about the interior than the exterior. It was a large, wooden building, one story, and made of the usual 1′ X 12′ boards.[9] The building faced east, its entrance on Avenue J and its stage at the opposite (west) end.[10] As far as can be determined, there was a center aisle, with seating on both sides. Individual chairs, whose number could be increased as needed, assured greater flexibility than benches. When dances were held in the house, the chairs were removed. On occasion, the chairs were loaned out, for example to Mayor Frank Wheelock for a party at his residence.[11]

Mary Howell wrote of the Opera House, "The drop curtains . . . were operated with ropes and were decorated with glamorous advertisements of local merchants. The 'drops' were let down between scenes and at intervals [intermission] so that the audience could read them." She adds that the building "was heated with coal stoves, one in the front and one in the back. Noisy lamps overhead hindered perfect hearing for the appreciative audience." And further, when a traveling company did not have sufficient properties, furniture stores in town loaned equipment in exchange for tickets.[12]

The house had one moving picture projector that showed crude, flickering silent movies. The projection booth was originally at the front of the building, where it obstructed the view, created unwanted noise, and was somewhat of a fire hazard. Hence, when the Opera House was remodeled in the fall of 1912, the booth was moved to the rear.[13] At first, electricity came from a gasoline generator, which provided enough power to operate the moving picture projector and fifty to sixty lights.[14] Later, electricity was obtained from the Lubbock Light and Ice Co. Since no theater would be complete without it, two enterprising citizens opened a confectionery store next door, known as the "Opera Confectionery."[15]

As a newly incorporated city, Lubbock faced the most ubiquitous of metropolitan struggles: taxation. Its long arm out-stretched, the City Council looked with enormous interest on the fledgling Orpheum Theatre, and it wasn't long before means were found for traveling companies to enrich both the citizens and the coffers of the city.[16] Now, the Opera House was ready to commence operation!

THE OPENING YEARS

During its first year, the Opera House proved a worthy successor to the Band Hall by hosting events of every stripe. It was much more than a play house and movie theater; excepting government functions and sporting events, virtually every other community activity, cultural and social, business and political, found its place there. A list of all known activities at the Opera House is given in Appendix B.

The structure had barely been completed when the Commercial Club Secretaries and Newspaper Men met there on April 21, 1909.[17] During May it saw use three times for the purpose of fund-raising: an ice cream supper for the benefit of the Woman's Home Mission Society; an "old-folks" concert for the benefit of the Presbyterian Church of Plainview; and a "big dance" to help out the Lubbock Baseball Team.[18] June events included the Woodmen of the World banquet, the Lubbock High School commencement exercises, and the Masons of Yellowhouse Lodge meeting.[19] And now, when various lecturers on religious subjects came to town, the Opera House with its capacity larger than any of the city's churches served as a religious meeting hall.

Also in its first year, it would be home to numerous concerts and recitals both by local talent, such as Nancy Patterson's and Lula Campbell's music classes, and traveling artists bringing vaudeville and dramatic productions to town. Perhaps its most community-oriented function that first year was for mass meetings or town councils, such as the one on February 16, 1910 that the newspaper referred to as a "love feast."[20] The main topic was the present state and future of the city, and several prominent citizens addressed the issue, including Judge John R. McGee, Mayor Frank E. Wheelock, O. L. Slaton, John J. Dillard, and W. H. Bledsoe. The newspaper ended its write-up of the meeting with an exhortation to the citizenry: "Let's get together and stay together." The Opera House was destined to play a role in helping the community toward that goal. Thus, the Opera House was to early Lubbock a multi-purpose facility that filled a wide variety of community needs, not unlike the present-day Memorial Civic Center.

Despite completion in April 1909, it was not until the initiation of passenger train service to Lubbock, after October 25, 1909, that it became practical for traveling companies to frequent the town. Hence, initial effort was concentrated on readying the motion picture equipment for the summer. In May a small generator was installed to power the projector.[21] Moving pictures quickly became established as the best entertainment in town, and by August were an every-night occurrence.

Charles Reppert managed the Orpheum at first, but as the time approached to book companies for the 1909–10 season, W. R. Payne was hired.[22] Bill Payne was nothing if not enterprising. He advertised himself as a "tonsorial artist" before selling his barber shop around the beginning of summer 1909. In August he and Ralph Penney opened a real estate office, the South Singer Land Company. By November he was managing the Opera House as well, and by the following June had gone into still another venture, manager of the Tremont Hotel.[23] Moreover, he was also a most colorful character. Lawrence Graves captured the spirit of the man well:

> Manager Payne was accustomed to advertise his attractions by riding his fine horse up and down the streets and shouting through a megaphone "Five hundred feet of movie film at the Opera House tonight." Wearing his pants tucked into shiny boots, with a long coat, large red bow tie, and tall silk hat, he invariably attracted the desired attention. At dusk he would stand in front of his theatre and shout through his megaphone.[24]

Mr. O. J. Davis remembers the very words: "Hurry, hurry, show starts right away." Payne in fact brought such gusto to the job that, within weeks, he deemed it necessary to print in the *Avalanche* a public apology for all the noise he was making:

I wish to notify the public in general that the reason and only reason I ballihoo for the Orpheum Opera House, is that it is in the interest of my business, and that at [any] time you have sick folks that it will bother, if you will kindly call me up by phone I will gladly desist.[25]

While parties in the home were frequent — the paper reported on a half dozen or so every week — parties were private affairs. Payne's goal was to try to reach the community with public entertainments of such kind and quality that the citizens would keep returning for more. Perhaps his biggest achievement during his first year was in bringing to town so many fine professional companies. The first for the 1909–1910 season was Angell's Comedians, who presented "The Duke's Daughter" on November 10 during a week's stay. Payne must have known he had satisfied a deep community need when he saw a full house each night and read a highly laudatory review in the newspaper:

> W. R. Payne, manager of the Orpheum House, is to be congratulated this week on having that ever interesting company Angel's Comedians with him for the week. So far [Thursday], they have played to a full and appreciative house, and for the remainder of the week will hold the boards at this attractive play house. Mr. Payne is bending every energy toward furnishing the theatre-goers with good companies, and in this company, he has made an exceptionally good hit.[26]

He responded to such encouragement with the Howard Stock Company for a week in late November, the Woodward Stock Company for three nights in December, and three vaudeville and dramatic companies, each for a week, in January. In February he featured Fred Raymond's comedy "The Missouri Girl," a play with musical numbers. It was billed as "positively the greatest fun event of the season," with first-class specialties and an outstanding cast.[27] The 1909–10 season found a total of ten companies at the Opera House. The rather eye-catching, handsome advertisement for "The Woods Sisters and their Excellent Company" is given in Figure 2. They were booked six days and presented a different play each performance, including "A Gay Deceiver," "Her Fatal Marriage," and "A Daughter of Dixie." Clearly, Payne was a successful operator, the Opera House was prospering, Lubbock's place on the itinerary of traveling companies was assured, and the community was enjoying more frequent doses of enlightenment or at least entertainment than it had ever known before.

That artistic activity voiced confidence in the future of the city was not lost on the new editor of the newspaper after 1908, James Dow, who made no secret of his pleasure at seeing the town thrive culturally.

Figure 2. Opera House advertisement for the Woods Sisters.
— The Lubbock Avalanche, April 28, 1910, p. 15.

Hence, he cooperated fully with the Opera House, regularly posting advertisements (usually one or two large boxed ads plus up to a half-dozen spot announcements scattered throughout the paper). Dow also printed advance publicity about the plays and the players, and wrote reviews, in which he indicated full and appreciative audiences most of the time and in which he invariably congratulated Payne for exceptional work done.

In addition to plays, moving pictures were presented on every available evening (except Sunday), with Saturday and other matinees as well. And here too, Payne sought out entertaining specialty acts. One of his noteworthy efforts was written up in the paper:

> Last Saturday evening, Arney Harbert, who is with the Orpheum Opera House [as equipment operator] at this place, gave quite a large crowd of spectators entertainment by sending into the air something modeled like an air ship. The passenger in this machine was a Tom Cat of a brindle color. After Mr. Cat had gotten up in the air something like 40 or 50 feet, a string was pulled letting him descend to the ground, the parachute opened nicely and the cat landed safe and sound on solid earth again.[28]

Payne also realized the benefit to his business of a certain amount of public service, and on occasion provided the house free of charge.

So, the Opera House got off to a running start its first year in operation with a full slate of musical, dramatic, and civic events. However, between September 1910 and September 1911, dramatic activity at the Opera House all but ceased. Only three troupes came to town during the entire season, compared to ten the previous year.[29]

While the reason is unknown, Bill Payne may have been a big part of the problem. One can imagine his loss of interest in the Opera House as his other interests, such as the Tremont Hotel (co-manager) and the South Singer Land Co. (co-owner) divided his energies. It is likely that his contract for the Opera House expired without renewal. Payne's brief tenure at the Opera House ended in early November 1911. Within a month, however, the Opera House was enjoying the services of a new manager, and the entertainment health of the community had begun to improve "dramatically."

THE ERVING McELROY YEARS

Erving M. McElroy arrived in Lubbock on December 14, 1911, to assume his new position as manager of the Opera House.[30] He would remain in Lubbock, although not in the theater business after the 1920's, for the rest of his life. McElroy approached the task with as much enthusiasm as his predecessor, but with more experience in the business, greater dedication, and better ideas of promotion. He quickly turned around the fortunes of the Opera House.

His first full season, 1912–13, saw at least nine companies come to town.[31] McElroy launched the 1913–14 season with a strategy designed to promote higher ticket sales and happier audiences, an advertisement of coming attractions for the season:[32]

COMING ATTRACTIONS
AT THE
OPERA HOUSE

Sept. 3rd and 4th	Mr. Oscar Graham
	"The Higher Law" and
	"A Prince of his Race"
Oct. 20th to 26th	The Dougherty Stock Co.
Nov. 10th to 16th	Angell's Comedians
Dec. 4th	"Sis Perkins"
Dec. 29th	"Sunbonnet Sue"
Jan. 17th	"The Thief"
Jan. 26th	"The Shepherd of the Hills"
Feb. 11th	"The Girl He Sent Away"

LYCEUM COURSE

Oct. 7th	The Chicago Ladies Orchestra
Oct. 27th	The Playsingers
Dec. 9th[33]	University Girls
Jan. 8th	Le Barge Music Co.
Mar. 13th	Brush the Great

Five more companies played later in the year, such as the United Play Co. and the Albert Taylor Company (twice), bringing the season total to eighteen, impressive testimony to the rapidly increasing cultural appetite of the young community.

That classical music was highly respected and in demand is demonstrated by the Lyceum Course. The five events of that season are indicative of the kind of music Lubbockites enjoyed from the annual Lyceum Course. The series opened with The Chicago Ladies Orchestra, billed as "the Lyceum's premier orchestral organization." "The entire personnel is made up of members of standing and marked ability, professional musicians capable of playing with the best musical organizations in America." The company lived up to its billing. So highly regarded was the concert that numerous encores were demanded before the audience would let the performers rest.[34]

Another Lyceum attraction followed just twenty days later. The Playsingers, billed as a "high-class lecture recital company," believed that music would be better appreciated if better understood. Hence, discussion preceded performance. The review indicated a splendid program, a large house, and a very appreciative audience. "The program was rendered with grace and ability and was enjoyed as no other ever presented in our city, especially by those who can properly appreciate classic music."[35] While not all Lyceum programs were of classical music, those that were always received an enthusiastic welcome from Lubbock audiences.

McElroy continually promoted and improved his operation, and he possessed a flair for truly creative ideas. One of the first, initiated just after his arrival on the scene, was a contest, whose prize was a solid stone clock hollowed out for the mechanism and with the entire face artistically hand-carved.[36] Next came a plan to erect an open-air theater for moving pictures during the summer months when the interior of the Opera House would be uncomfortably hot. Located at the north side of the square near the northeast corner of Main Street and Texas Avenue, the Airdome opened in May 1912. Like most airdomes of the day, the front, housing the projection booth, was enclosed, while the rest was open to the evening sky, thus anticipating today's drive-in movie theater. The Airdome showed movies every night through the summer of 1912 and again in 1913 (see advertisement below, p. 85).[37]

A few days after the Airdome opened, McElroy hosted the formation of the Western Cooperative Theatrical Association, which covered West Texas and included in a circuit the towns of Tulia, Plainview, Lubbock, Snyder, Sweetwater, and Coleman (all connected by the Santa Fe Railroad). Its main purpose was to ensure high quality and to raise the "moral theatrical standard" for the West Texas audience.[38]

One brilliantly-conceived proposition, put in place in the fall of 1912, brought him into collaboration with a dozen of the town's merchants, who purchased, and then gave away free to their customers, tickets to the Saturday matinee each week. According to the weekly notice in the newspaper, the plan worked as follows:

Every man, woman and child, old and young, are invited to call on the following merchants between the hours of 8 a.m. and 3 p.m. every Saturday beginning Oct. 19th and receive free tickets to the Matinee of Moving Pictures at the Opera House.[39]

This promotion was aimed mainly at farmers and their families, providing just one more incentive for a Saturday trip to town. Everyone involved came out a winner: the farmers, the businessmen, and the Opera House.

Perhaps the best evidence of the depth of cultural interest in Lubbock was the need to enlarge the house after only three years in operation. During the fall of 1912, McElroy oversaw the project which included expanding the building (to the rear) to increase the stage 150 square feet and the seating capacity to 450, adding new scenery, repapering the walls, repainting the advertising curtain, and moving the projection booth to the back of the theater, out of harm's way.[40]

Yet another crowd-pleaser that McElroy's son Roy remembers was the time his father hired Bomar Moore, the town's champion wrestler, to wrestle a muzzled bear on the stage.[41] Makes one wonder what other specialty acts McElroy secured!

Finally, one cannot help but admire a man who selflessly and with considerable ingenuity bent his energies toward solving one of the town's thorniest problems: not crime, not poverty, not flooded streets after a rain, but flies. He devised what may be the all-time novel approach, involving an admission offer to the movies no youngster could refuse and a solution to a nuisance every citizen could applaud. The newspaper provided full details:

> This is his plan: Friday morning from 10 to 11 o'clock a.m., July 3rd, he proposes to run his picture show of high-grade pictures and will admit, absolutely free, every child between the ages of one year and thirty-five, who brings with them 100 or more dead flies.
>
> McElroy requested us to state that no one would be admitted carrying live flies with them, so it is important that you have them "dead" before presenting them at the picture show ticket station.[42]

Among McElroy's many creative ideas was one that proves puzzling for today's readers of the early newspaper notices. Shortly after his arrival, advertisements appeared for the Opera House as well as a place called the Lyric Theatre. For example, the January 25, 1912, paper contained a notice of a performance by local talent in the Opera House. On March 7, a notice heralded moving pictures at the Lyric Theatre. Were the Lyric Theatre and the Opera House two different theaters? The November 21, 1912, paper suggests an explanation; it includes advertisements for a single event at both places at the same time. There could be only one theater!

Perhaps what McElroy was attempting to do, then, was to distinguish not two separate theaters but two different functions of a single theater. A check of all the theater advertising for 1912–1913 shows, in general, that the "Lyric Theatre" was the name used to announce moving pictures, while the "Opera House" name was used for plays or other live performances.[43]

Probably McElroy implemented the system in order to make clear whether the house was featuring a movie or a play, a distinction perhaps unclear from the title alone. In any case, the dual practice ended when McElroy leased another theater, located on the west side of the square and which he named the Lyric, in the late summer of 1913.[44]

Evidently by that time Lubbock had entirely outgrown a single theater. Moving pictures had become immensely popular throughout the country and in Lubbock as well. But how could McElroy satisfy the movie-going public on those evenings when other events occupied the house, such as a play company holding the boards for an entire week, as was frequently the case? The answer was a second theater.[45] With two theaters, he could print the following policy statement in the paper, finally putting the matter to rest:

NOTICE

I wish to state to the public that the Picture Show will run every night, rain or shine. No attraction at the Opera House will conflict in any way with the daily program at the Lyric Theatre.

All attractions at the Opera House will be advertised under name of Opera House, and all moving picture attractions under head of Lyric Theatre.[46]

In summary, Erving McElroy took seriously his position as manager of the Opera House and brought to it enthusiasm, ingenuity, and ability. He booked touring companies, musicians, moving pictures, and specialty acts. He scheduled local events, donated the facility for community service projects on some occasions, and rented it out on others. He formed an organization with fellow theater managers, and screened productions for appropriate moral character. He oversaw the needed expansion of the Opera House, constructed the Airdome, the summer open-air theater, and, beginning September 1913, operated two full-time theaters, the Lyric and the Opera House. McElroy devised cooperative enterprises with the local merchants and was continually on the lookout for ways to improve business as well as service. He was one busy manager and one of the town's most caring citizens.

Unavailable issues of the newspaper from July 9, 1914 through August 22, 1918 (the World War I years) shield from investigation the activities of the Opera House during that period. By 1918 there was no more Opera House. Instead, plays were presented in the recently-built Lindsey Theatre, while movies were shown at the Lyric. The Opera House building may well have been torn down or moved; a wooden building so close to the center of town would have been somewhat of an anachronism in 1918. Whatever its fate, it served the community well. From the moment of its completion in April 1909, it was, so to speak, where the cultural action was.

Thus, Lubbock's Opera House was typical of similar theaters dotting the nation's rural landscape, to which the town still belonged. Whether melodrama, comedy, vaudeville, or even Shakespeare (Hilliard Wright and Company brought "Hamlet" to Lubbock in January 1913), Lubbock's citizens responded enthusiastically with their applause and their dollars. What they couldn't know at the time that the Band Hall and Opera House were in operation was that the traveling dramatic repertory company movement had already passed its peak and was about to lose a fatal challenge from the nascent movie, radio, and recording industries. But Lubbock audiences would nonetheless enjoy several more good years of repertory theater before the movement was over.

CHAPTER 4

The Municipal Bands, Part I:
The Original Band and The Lubbock 1906 Band*

During the second half of the nineteenth century and the first two decades of the twentieth, bands were the most conspicuous feature on the country's musical landscape. While a community might not have a symphony orchestra or even a chamber ensemble, it almost always boasted a brass band. At the peak of the movement local bands numbered as many as twenty thousand.[1] In most small communities, the only instrumental concert music the citizens heard, aside from that presented in church or in the home, was provided by the band, making the fifteen to twenty member band the most visible and audible musical organization of the day. And in addition to town bands there were factory bands, miners' bands, farmers' bands, ethnic and nationalistic bands, women's bands, children's bands, family bands, men's club (Elks, Odd Fellows, Masons, etc.) bands, prison bands, military bands, veterans' bands, circus bands, professional concert bands — in short, bands for almost every segment of American society.[2]

THE BAND MOVEMENT IN AMERICA

Men like Patrick Gilmore (1829–1892) and John Philip Sousa (1854–1932) helped to establish the band throughout the United States as the public entertainment medium *par excellence*. Sousa's fabulous career established him as the greatest musical attraction America had yet produced; his legacy includes a world-famous band, an incomparable group of compositions (marches) for band, and an influence still undiminished in the high school and college band movement.[3]

Bands could be found performing on just about any occasion where music was desirable: for Fourth of July celebrations, agricultural fairs, temperence rallies, picnics, openings of railroads, official openings of new towns, excursion and other parties, political rallies, dances, parades, weddings, funerals, welcoming dignitaries — the list is almost limitless. And they might even play for no other reason than to entertain the home folks.

A town's eagerness for a band is dramatized in Meredith Willson's "The Music Man," in which townspeople will believe even a slick charlatan who promises them a band. Why such popularity? Perhaps the Rudolph Wurlitzer Company summed it up best in the apt observation: "There is nothing that rouses the universal enthusiasm of everybody as does a spirited band."[4] As a consequence, "Americans across the country contributed generously to the support of bands and congregated enthusiastically, often by the thousands, to hear the bands play."[5] As baseball came to be the sport of the people, so band music came to be the music of the people. Band music reached out and touched thousands upon thousands of ordinary Americans; until around the time of World War I, it was truly the music of the masses.

Players' enthusiasm provided another reason for the popularity of bands. An aspiring bandsman could join a band without experience, even without musical knowledge. Moreover, the instruments were relatively inexpensive, were not terribly difficult to learn to play, and the usual band arrangements did not make especially great demands upon the players. Since musical ability was not a prerequisite for most hometown bands, a not inconsiderable burden of teaching, as well as directing, fell upon the band leader, who had to be rather proficient on most of the instruments, a good if not superb musician, and perhaps above all a man of inordinate patience. Yet, with daily practice by the bandsmen at home, frequent group rehearsals, and the most capable players on the leading parts, the director could whip into shape a successful musical team in as little as sixty days. But those first few sessions must have made many a band director want to leave town:

Judging from the number of contemporary jokes about the inelegant sounds of a beginning band, these first "noises" could not have been easy on the neighbors. One of the many popular gags, published in *The Leader* in 1885, defined a "band of mercy" as "a brass band that didn't practice evenings." Another often repeated one-liner proclaimed that the evil that men do lives after them because "when an amateur [bands-man] dies, he leaves the fatal instrument behind."[6]

Regarding the typical instrumental composition of bands, brass instruments dominated, sometimes to the complete exclusion of woodwinds, rounded out by a small percussion battery. Lubbock's bands, however, included two or three woodwinds, thereby providing a greater variety of tone, contrast of timbre, and warmth of sound than is characteristic of an all-brass ensemble. The (non-percussion) instruments were usually considered in terms of range:

soprano (piccolo, flutes, clarinets, trumpets, cornets): either about 3′
    (E♭) or about 5′ (B♭) in length of tube
alto (alto trombone, alto horns): about 7′ in length (E♭)
tenor/baritone (tenor trombones, baritone horns, euphoniums): about 9′
    in length (B♭)
bass (tuba): about 13′ in length (E♭)[7]

After the purchase of instruments and instruction in the fundamentals came, on the long road from inception to premier performance, the selection of music. Here the band director had an immense repertoire to choose from: marches, patriotic songs such as "Hail, Columbia," or "The Star-Spangled Banner," popular songs including Stephen Foster favorites, and programmatic pieces such as "Battle of Trenton" or "An Alpine Storm." Dances (waltzes, quadrilles, polkas, gallops, quick-steps) and transcriptions from the Classics (overtures especially, operatic selections too) also found interpretation.

With instruments, instruction, and music taken care of, the next item of concern was uniforms; in many cases, acquisition of stylish uniforms was only slightly less important than the other items. As M. and R. Hazen stated,

> Such a situation is conjured up in *The Music Man* when River City's un-flappable bandmaster, Professor Harold Hill, faced with inquiries about his ability to form a band, quips lightly, "When the uniforms arrive they'll forget about everything else." It is a comic line but, as writer Meredith Willson knew from his many years with the Sousa Band, it bore a clear relationship to historical reality.[8]

Finally comes publicity, attracting the crowd to the concert. Perhaps this was a problem in some places but none at all in Lubbock, where, if word of mouth didn't reach everyone, the numerous announcements and programs in the newspaper, courtesy of editor and No. 1 fan James

Dow, did. Our story of Lubbock's bands begins appropriately with Dow, who, like other newspaper editors in towns across the country, saw the band as vital to growth and development and who often wrote powerful editorials on its behalf.

A BAND FOR LUBBOCK

"Why Not a Band?" That question led off an impassioned essay in the September 30, 1909 *Lubbock Avalanche* exhorting the citizens of Lubbock to support a band. The eloquence and intensity with which Editor Dow put forth the need proved successful, and within three months the paper, with great pride and best wishes for success, announced the formation of a civic band. This was not, however, the only such plea the people of Lubbock would read in their newspaper over the years, for the early history of Lubbock's bands resembled a roller coaster ride: many ups and downs, with occasional derailments. Nor was the band formed in December 1909 Lubbock's first band; it was the third. For the first, one has to return to late 1904 or early 1905.

From late 1904 or early 1905 through the coming of the railroad to Lubbock in 1909 and the end of the town's geographical isolation, one of the major avenues of culture and entertainment was the band. In an interview conducted on June 25, 1958 by Jean A. Paul for the Texas Tech University Southwest Collection, Smylie C. Wilson recounted the founding of Lubbock's first civic band:

> That picture of the band I showed you the other night was taken in 1905. The band had been organized for some time before that. I believe we brought it into being in the latter part of 1904. At the latest it was the early part of 1905 . . . When I brought out my slide trombone it was quite a curiosity. I don't think many of them had ever seen a musical instrument before . . . Interest developed in the possibility of organizing a town band, and it just "growed like Topsy."[9]

Wilson provided a guiding hand in the formation of the band and was its first director as well. Instruments were purchased from the Conn Music Company, one of the best-known in the country at the time, and each member owned his own instrument.[10] Wilson described the band's musical repertoire: "A great deal of the music we played was march music. We played the popular band music of the day. We played some waltzes from time to time, some overtures, but nothing fancy."[11] That modest description is substantiated by occasional programs of band concerts printed in *The Avalanche*. Moreover, according to Wilson, "No one had to try out [for the band]. If you wanted to play, you bought an instrument and came down and made noise for a while until you could make music."[12] Under the circumstances, the standard of playing could not have been very high, and progress must have been painfully slow. Perhaps to compensate for their musical limitations and to fill out concerts that typically contained no more than three or four numbers by the band, the bandsmen put on plays. Wilson was very proud of the musical and theatrical efforts of the band, for in the days before the coming of the railroad, it was the town's primary entertainment resource.[13]

Another source for Lubbock's first band gives this fascinating account:

> In the latter part of 1904 or the early part of 1905, several Lubbock citizens formed a band under the direction of Smylie C. Wilson.
>
> Those who composed the band were: J. J. Dillard, the tuba; C. E. Hunt, tenor horn; W. M. Crawford, valve trombone; N. W. Crawford, baritone; Lambert Wilson, bass drum; Lehman Wilson and his younger brother, the clarinets; a Mr. McDonald, the snare drum; and others.
>
> One night early in 1905 when the band was scheduled to play a concert at Plainview, a wild bull charged a car driven by Sylvanus Turkenkopf and containing several band members. It required a great deal of time and patience to extricate the car from the carcass of the bull, delaying part of the band. The waiting audience at Plainview thought there would be no concert. However, after hope had almost vanished, the band arrived, much disheveled, and gave a very entertaining concert.[14]

Oh, what hardships to suffer! Nonetheless, the account confirms the establishment of Lubbock's first band in late 1904 or early 1905. Furthermore, besides proving that in 1905 a bull was no match for a car, it provides a list of bandmembers. To the eight mentioned with instruments should be added Smylie Wilson, trombone, and Sylvannus Turkenkopf, piccolo.

There is evidence suggesting that Lubbock's first band led a rather brief existence. It faced one insurmountable problem: no band teacher to instruct the beginners how to play their instruments or even how to read musical notation. Without such help, the band could scarcely have succeeded. Nevertheless, the effort was not wasted; a seed had been sown, and from the ashes of the original band arose, sometime in 1906, Lubbock's second band.

THE LUBBOCK 1906 BAND

The name itself as well as a banner across the bass drum confirm the year of origin. The precise date is unknown,[15] but the Lubbock 1906 Band must have been in existence before November, for *The Lubbock Leader,* which began publication November 15, 1906, contained in its premier issue an announcement of a concert by the band.[16]

Although Smylie Wilson seems not to have remembered two distinct bands, information about the Lubbock 1906 Band comes from three other primary sources. The first is a photograph of the band together with identifications; the second, an advertisement for the Lubbock 1906 Band listing its personnel; and the third, the available record of the newspapers from the period in question.

The well-known photograph of the band standing in front of the Band Hall is reproduced in Plate 3. A copy in the Texas Tech University Southwest Collection as well as one in the Texas Tech Museum are accompanied by an identification list, perhaps by Smylie Wilson. The photo may even be the one referred to above by Wilson (p. 34); but a date of 1905 is definitely too early. First, there is another, nearly identical but less well-known photo (Plate 4) taken immediately before or after the one in Plate 3, and subsequently used for a postcard where it bears the caption: "After rendering 'Dixie,' July 4th, 1907, Lubbock, Texas."[17] Second, a rather old copy — perhaps the original — of Plate 3, now in the Texas Tech Museum, bears on the back the same date.[18] Hence, the photo in Plate 3 must have been taken on July 4, 1907.

Apparently almost all the original band members joined the Lubbock 1906 Band:

Plate 3. The Lubbock 1906 Band.
— Photo courtesy Southwest Collection, Texas Tech
University, Lubbock, Texas

Plate 4. The Lubbock 1906 Band.
After rendering "Dixie," July 4th, 1907, Lubbock, Texas
— Photo courtesy Museum, Texas Tech University,
Lubbock, Texas

Standing, left to right:	Sylvanns C. Turkenkopf, piccolo
	G. L. Lister, clarinet
	— clarinet
	Will Ross, euphonium
	Marion M. Crawford, valve tenor trombone
	Will Crawford, slide alto trombone
	Zeb Agnew, helicon
	Mason, valve alto trombone
	J. J. Dillard, tuba
	Ed Green, alto horn
	Smylie C. Wilson, slide tenor trombone
	McDonald, baritone
	Walter Custis, baritone
Kneeling, left to right:	Jennings Winn, cornet
	Luther (Jack) Caldwell, cornet
	Lambert Wilson, bass drum
	Lehman Wilson, snare drum
	Ed Carlock, cornet
	J. L. Dow, cornet

These identifications are not all certain, and at least two corrections can be made. Ed Carlock was not in Lubbock at the time, but W. B. Leeman was. Also, Clifford Hunt's relatives identified him in the place of Mr. McDonald.[19]

The second source for the Lubbock 1906 Band is a document entitled "Souvenir Edition of 'Eleanor Waltzes,'" boosting the town of Lubbock and evidently intended for circulation nationwide. Examination of the document leads to a date around September 1907.[20] It consists of a musical composition, "Eleanor Waltzes" by William B. Leeman, an employee of *The Avalanche,* presented, according to a notice at the head of the music, "Compliments of the Business Men of Lubbock, Texas, 'Queen City of the Staked Plains.'" The composition is encased in a cover, the outside front (Figure 3) and back (Figure 4) of which contain advertising by those businessmen. The inside front (Figure 5) provides "Facts About Lubbock" (the inside back is blank). One of those ads is for the Lubbock 1906 Band listing its membership (Figure 4, lower left).

Figure 6 presents the two lists of bandsmen allowing us to get a more accurate picture of the make-up of this band:

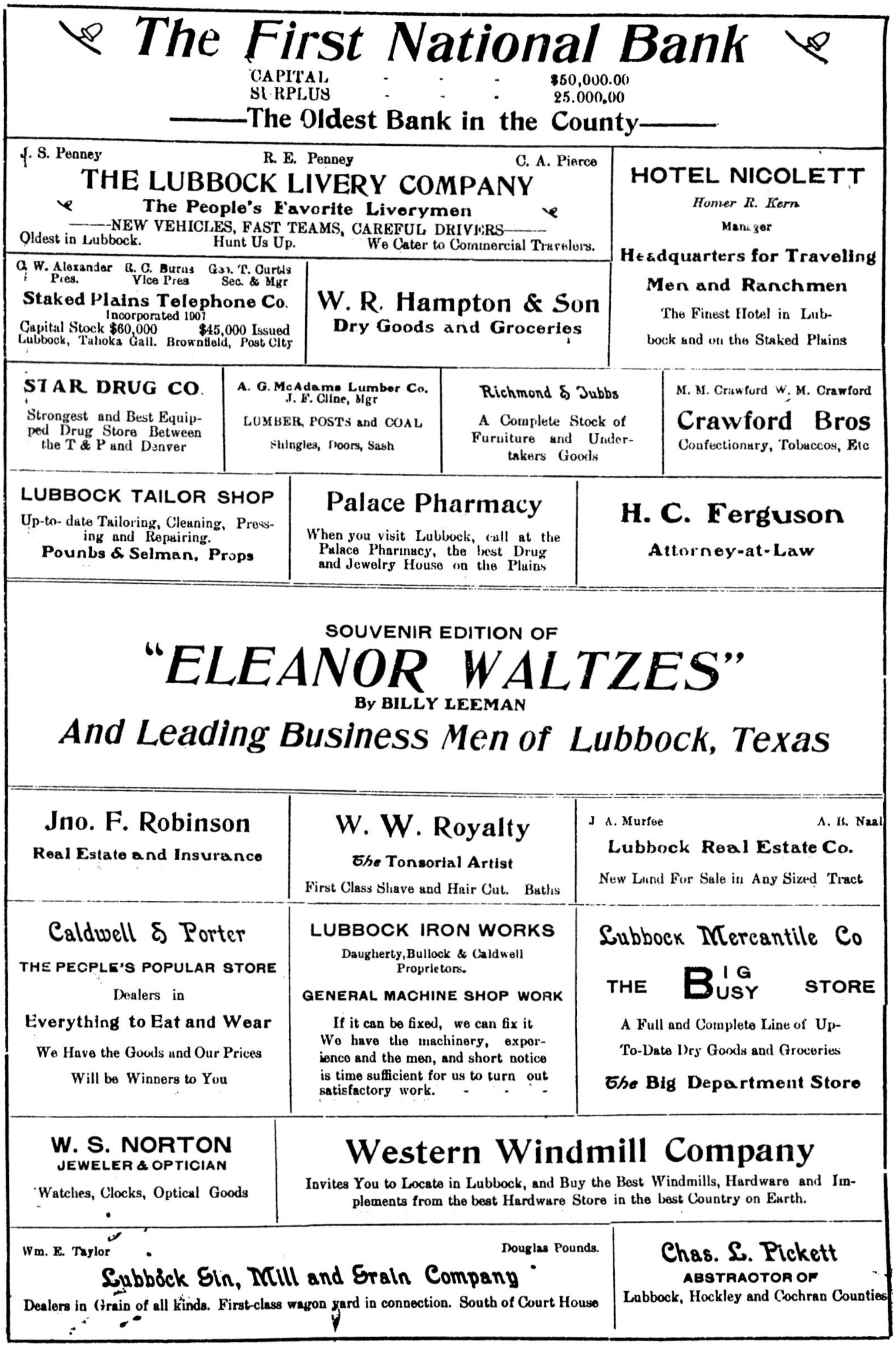

The First National Bank

CAPITAL - - - - $50,000.00

SURPLUS - - - - 25,000.00

——The Oldest Bank in the County——

J. S. Penney R. E. Penney C. A. Pierce

THE LUBBOCK LIVERY COMPANY

The People's Favorite Liverymen

——NEW VEHICLES, FAST TEAMS, CAREFUL DRIVERS——

Oldest in Lubbock. Hunt Us Up. We Cater to Commercial Travelers.

HOTEL NICOLETT

Homer R. Kern

Manager

Headquarters for Traveling Men and Ranchmen

The Finest Hotel in Lubbock and on the Staked Plains

G. W. Alexander, Pres. R. C. Burns, Vice Pres. Geo. T. Curtis, Sec. & Mgr

Staked Plains Telephone Co.

Incorporated 1907

Capital Stock $60,000 $45,000 Issued

Lubbock, Tahoka, Gail, Brownfield, Post City

W. R. Hampton & Son

Dry Goods and Groceries

STAR DRUG CO.

Strongest and Best Equipped Drug Store Between the T & P and Denver

A. G. McAdams Lumber Co.

J. F. Cline, Mgr

LUMBER, POSTS and COAL

Shingles, Doors, Sash

Richmond & Dubbs

A Complete Stock of Furniture and Undertakers Goods

M. M. Crawford W. M. Crawford

Crawford Bros

Confectionary, Tobaccos, Etc

LUBBOCK TAILOR SHOP

Up-to-date Tailoring, Cleaning, Pressing and Repairing.

Pounbs & Selman, Props

Palace Pharmacy

When you visit Lubbock, call at the Palace Pharmacy, the best Drug and Jewelry House on the Plains

H. C. Ferguson

Attorney-at-Law

SOUVENIR EDITION OF

"ELEANOR WALTZES"

By BILLY LEEMAN

And Leading Business Men of Lubbock, Texas

Jno. F. Robinson

Real Estate and Insurance

W. W. Royalty

The Tonsorial Artist

First Class Shave and Hair Cut. Baths

J. A. Murfee A. B. Neal

Lubbock Real Estate Co.

New Land For Sale in Any Sized Tract

Caldwell & Porter

THE PEOPLE'S POPULAR STORE

Dealers in

Everything to Eat and Wear

We Have the Goods and Our Prices Will be Winners to You

LUBBOCK IRON WORKS

Daugherty, Bullock & Caldwell Proprietors.

GENERAL MACHINE SHOP WORK

If it can be fixed, we can fix it. We have the machinery, experience and the men, and short notice is time sufficient for us to turn out satisfactory work.

Lubbock Mercantile Co

THE BIG BUSY STORE

A Full and Complete Line of Up-To-Date Dry Goods and Groceries

The Big Department Store

W. S. NORTON

JEWELER & OPTICIAN

Watches, Clocks, Optical Goods

Western Windmill Company

Invites You to Locate in Lubbock, and Buy the Best Windmills, Hardware and Implements from the best Hardware Store in the best Country on Earth.

Wm. E. Taylor Douglas Pounds.

Lubbock Gin, Mill and Grain Company

Dealers in Grain of all kinds. First-class wagon yard in connection. South of Court House

Chas. L. Pickett

ABSTRACTOR OF

Lubbock, Hockley and Cochran Counties

Figure 3. "Eleanor Waltzes": Cover.

— Photo courtesy Southwest Collection, Texas Tech University, Lubbock, Texas

W. H. Vaughn H. B. Earnest

VAUGHN & EARNEST

LIVERY, FEED AND SALE STABLE

WHEN YOU NEED OUR SERVICE PHONE NO. 30

GOOD TEAMS AND RIGS AND FAST DRIVERS

THE PLAINS LUMBER & GRAIN CO

LUMBER, GRAIN AND COAL

Yards at

LUBBOCK, PLAINVIEW, TULIA and HAPPY

PENNEY, PICKET & BURNS

General Land Agents

WRITE US FOR INFORMATION

GEO. L. BEATTY

LAWYER

Lubbock Racket Store

A COMPLETE LINE OF RACKET GOODS

R. T. Penney W. O. Kincannon

Penney & Kincannon

BARBERS

Bean & Martin

LAWYERS.

H. R. Mason H. L Gibson

Mason & Gibson

Contractors & Builders

Meat Market and Bakery

Sanders & Sanders

Choice Meats. First Class Bakery Goods

R. A. RANKIN & SON

Hardware, Implements and Groceries

GENERAL BLACKSMITH SHOP

J. B. Martin, Prop

Iron and Woodworkman

J. J. Dillard, Lawyer Ed Green, Notary Public W. B Powell, Notary Public

Dillard-Powell Land Company

Show the most complete list offarm and ranch property in Lubbock and adjoining counties from $10 to $20 and from 80 acres up. Without a doubt we show you the best proposition on the market. Correspondence solicted. Courtesies extended real estate men.

LUBBOCK 1906 BAND

C. H. Lister, Clarinet W. B. Powell, Clarinet S. C. Turkenkoph Piccolo

W. B. Leeman, Solo Cornet, S. L. Dow, Solo Cornet, H. B. Sarnest, 1st Cornet, J. Caldwell and J. Winn, 2nd Cornets, W Crawford, H. R. Mason, Ed Green, altos S. Wilson, W. Custis, Trombones, J. J. Dillard, Z. Vgnew, M. Crawford, Basses L. Wilson and J. D. D. Quick, Drums

Hartford Land Co.

GENERAL REAL ESTATE DEALERS

Will Send you a map and price list. Write for them and when here make us a call. Improved and unimproved land for sale.

The Avalanche

The best paper in the county Try a copy.

The Best equipped plant in the West

INVEST IN LUBBOCK PROPERTY

The Overton Addition to the town of Lubbock joins the old part or town on the west and is rapidly filling up with nice homes. Lots fifty feet wide, wide streets and alleys. Invest now and get the benefit of advance in prices. Write for map, prices, etc.

DR. M. C. OVERTON

Figure 4. "Eleanor Waltzes": Cover.

Facts About Lubbock.

Lubbock, the county site, a thriving town of 900 population, is situated in the center of the county on the forks of the Yellow House Canyon, (Brazos River) 125 miles south of Amarillo on the Denver Railway, 45 miles south of Plainview on the A. T. & Santa Fe and 125 miles north of Big Springs on the T. & P. Luebbock has two National Banks, two hotels, three daily mails, an excellent school and building, a $5,000 gin, 'a fine teledhone exhange, local and long distance connections; 50 business firms, 12 real estate firms, 9 lawyers, 4 physicians, 1 dentist, 2 incorporated abstract companies, 4 church buildings, two blacksmith shops, one iron works and machine shop, two lumber yards, two livery barns, two papers, daily auto line to Plainview, which runs two small cars and a 16-passenger car. It offers superior advantages to the home-seeker, health-seeker and to the investor. Good water, and land that will produce anything. The Panhandle Short Line, Roswell and Eastern railroads have been surveyed here and are a certainty.

LUBBOCK WANTS

An electric light plant, steam laundry, ice plant, cement block factory, compress, flour mill, oil mill, 10,-000 families to settle in the city, 15,000 tillers of the soil to locate in Lubbock County, all good people in the United States to settle here and enjoy life with us in this beautiful country. There is always room for one more. : :

Figure 5. "Eleanor Waltzes": Cover.

FIGURE 6

July 4, 1907 Photograph	Souvenir Edition of Eleanor Waltzes: September 1907[a]
Zeb Agnew, helicon	Z. Agnew, bass[b]
Luther (Jack) Caldwell, cornet	J. Caldwell, 2nd cornet
Marion M. Crawford, valve tenor trombone	M. Crawford, bass
Will Crawford, slide alto trombone	W. Crawford, alto
Walter Custis, baritone	W. Custis, trombone
J. J. Dillard, tuba	J. J. Dillard, bass
J. L. Dow, cornet	J. L. Dow, solo cornet
	H. B. Earnest, 1st cornet
Ed Green, alto horn	Ed Green, alto
W. B. Leeman, cornet	W. B. Leeman, solo cornet
G. L. Lister, clarinet[c]	C. H. Lister, clarinet
Mason, valve alto trombone	H. R. Mason, alto
Clifford Hunt, baritone	
— clarinet	W. B. Powell, clarinet
	J. D. Quick, drums
Will Ross, euphonium	S. C. Turkenkopf, piccolo
Sylvanns C. Turkenkopf, piccolo	L. Wilsons, drums
Lambert Wilson, bass drum	
Lehman Wilson, snare drum	S. Wilson, trombone
Smylie C. Wilson, slide tenor trombone	J. Winn, 2nd cornet
Jennings Winn, cornet	

[a] *Several typographical errors have been corrected*

[b] *Some of the brass are listed simply as alto or bass*

[c] *C. H. is correct*

The members of the Lubbock 1906 Band numbered among the town's leading citizens for the most part, professional and trades men who brought commerce as well as culture to Lubbock. J. J. Dillard edited *The Avalanche* from its founding in May 1900 to April 1908; he was also a real estate promoter, lawyer, judge, and, in 1910, State Representative. W. B. Powell was a realtor and owner, along with Dillard, of the Dillard–Powell Land Co. James L. Dow had served as associate editor of *The Avalanche* since January 1906 and took over as editor upon Dillard's departure from the paper in April 1908. Jennings Winn was the son of a minister; Luther Jack Caldwell, the son of one of the town's leading merchants. The Crawford brothers, Marion and Will, owned a confectionery and tobacco store and were jewelers as well, with Will Crawford serving many years as County Treasurer. J. D. Quick managed Plains Lumber and Grain Company. Smylie Wilson managed the Western Windmill Co. H. R. Mason was a contractor and builder. H. B. Earnest co-owned the Vaughn & Earnest Livery, Feed, and Sale Stable. Lambert Wilson drove for the Dillard–Powell Land Co. Ed Green too worked for Dillard–Powell, serving as notary public. W. B. Leeman and C. H. Lister both worked at *The Avalanche*. Zeb Agnew was a builder. Although six men have a connection with J. J. Dillard, the band seemed not to have had any planned or particular make-up; Dillard merely got everyone he could to join.

What brought these eighteen or nineteen men together to form a band and to contribute the time and effort that one requires? First of all, they must have appreciated the role a band can play in promoting the city. If they didn't come to that appreciation on their own, J. J. Dillard and James Dow helped, repeatedly using the newspaper to promote Lubbock, via the band, to outsiders and visitors. Witness the following statements: "As has been stated in this connection before, the Lubbock Band is purely a public benefactor. It was organized for the purpose of helping to build up the town and every one is bound to admit that it has been the source of much favorable comment from visitors."[21] "We are apt to have many distinguished men visiting these parts and what could be more appropriate than to meet them at the depot with a well organized and well trained band."[22] "Why not the citizens of the town send the Lubbock Band to Dallas during the State Fair? It would be a great advertisement for the town that could not be done so effectually any other way."[23]

Second, since growth of the city could only be positive for the business climate, the businessmen in the band were investing in their own future as well as that of their city. Moreover, the band also offered congenial fellowship and an avenue to all-around personal enrichment. However, civic pride, commercial self-interest, and even personal enrichment do not tell the whole story where music is concerned. People also form bands for the sheer pleasure of making music for themselves and for the indescribable joy derived from entertaining others, reasons surely not absent here.

CHRONICLE OF ACTIVITIES

One would also like to know how much time and effort the bandsmen expended in the pursuit of their goals. What problems, if any, did they encounter? What were their expenses? From where did financial support come? How were they received by the community? Where did they perform? How often? What music? When did the Lubbock 1906 Band come to its end, and why? At least partial answers to these and other questions may be obtained from the principal source of information regarding the activities of the band, *The Avalanche.*

To promote the success of the band as far as they were able, the editors of *The Avalanche* devoted what can only be described as an extraordinary amount of space to covering the band's activities and to educating the citizens both to the band's function as town booster as well as to the community's role in the band's support. The first concert of which there is record in *The Avalanche* took place on August 10, 1907. The program, one of only two extant, is reproduced in Figure 7. The other program, from November 8, is given in Figure 9. From all available evidence, both appear to be representative and reveal much about the band's concerts. First of all, non-band members participated; the concerts provided a stage for all Lubbock's musically and theatrically talented citizens. Second, the band itself played only three or four numbers, comprising a rather small portion of the program; but that was all that could reasonably be expected from the group, given its limited repertoire and experience. Third, part of each program consisted of solo performances of various kinds. And finally, the band excelled in presenting minstrels, vaudevilles, and farces. Especially delightful, according to the newspaper, was "Cato, Leb and Col. Spruceup" (Figure 9), a "side-splitting and button busting farce" overflowing with laughable features.[24] Such concerts were truly variety shows with a great diversity of programming, involving members of the band and talented members of the community as well. The band seems to have been a catalyst galvanizing the community

PROGRAMME

1. Donator March - - - - Band
2. Duett—Cornet and Baritone. "Home Sweet Home." Winn and Ross.
3. D. H. S. March - - - - Band
4. Recitation - - - Miss Jarrott.
5. Quartette—Vocal. S. C. Wilson, L. C. Wilson. W. A. Custis, Z. D. Agnew.
6. Victor March - - - - Band
7. Piano Solo - - - Miss McGee.
8. Recitation - - - Miss Nevels.
9. Trombone Solo : - - S. C. Wilson
10. Farce—"Jumbo Jum." Characters: Gobbleton, S. C. Turkenkoph; Hannah, Miss Phenix; Mrs. Gobbleton, Mrs. E. B. Green; Lawyer Cheatham. H. R. Mason; Adelaide, Miss McLarry; Henry Merrille. Z. D. Agnew; "Jumbo Jum" S. C. Wilson.
11 Henry Brown. Comic Black-face. S. C. Wilson

Figure 7. Lubbock 1906 Band Program.
— The Avalanche, August 9, 1907, p. 6.

into providing its own entertainment and diversion.

The next concert took place on October 19. One can now clearly detect a growing sense of urgency about the band's financial condition. In a lengthy article the newspaper exhorted the citizens of Lubbock to support their band, saying, "other towns have to pay men to play, furnish them with instruments, music and uniforms and then do not have as good a band as we have."[25] The paper even went so far as to print a huge advertisement for the concert (Figure 8), sure to catch the eye of its readers. While the paper hoped, through its efforts, to help the band generate enough ticket sales to match expenses, inclement weather on the night of the concert kept hope from becoming reality. The review of the concert indicated a good audience but not a full house.[26]

For the next concert, then, *The Avalanche* increased its promotional effort, with a longer, more informative, and more urgent article aimed at educating the community to the purpose of the band and the cost of maintaining it.[27] The financial facts were laid squarely on the table: the treasury was empty, and the band had to take in at least $60 to $70 to meet monthly expenses such as hall rent and instructor's fees.[28] In addition, the paper printed the complete program (Figure 9) and yet another reminder not to miss the concert.[29] Clearly, the paper was doing everything it reasonably could to boost the fortunes of the band. Did the effort succeed? We do not know. The review of the concert contained only two sentences, neither giving any hint of the financial returns, although such uncharacteristic brevity might be taken as a discouraging sign.[30] But help was on the way; an angel in the wings was about to make her appearance. The November 29 *Avalanche* (p. 1) announced that "Miss Patterson's Music Class gave an entertainment on last Monday night which was quite a success and well received. The proceeds of the entertainment were donated to the Lubbock 1906 Band."

It must have been gratifying, perhaps lifesaving, for the band to receive help from one of the town's music teachers. That circumstances now retreated from the critical level may be surmised from another notice in the November 29 issue. The band had completed arrangements to lease for another year the Band Hall, where their rehearsals took place and the concerts were given, and, furthermore, had contracted a painter to paint back and side scenes on the stage of the hall.

The January 3, 1908 *Avalanche* had nothing but good news to bear. A play put on around Christmas time yielded gross receipts of $123.40, which should have done much to fill the coffers of the Band's treasury; in addition, the band had just elected new officers for 1908.[31]

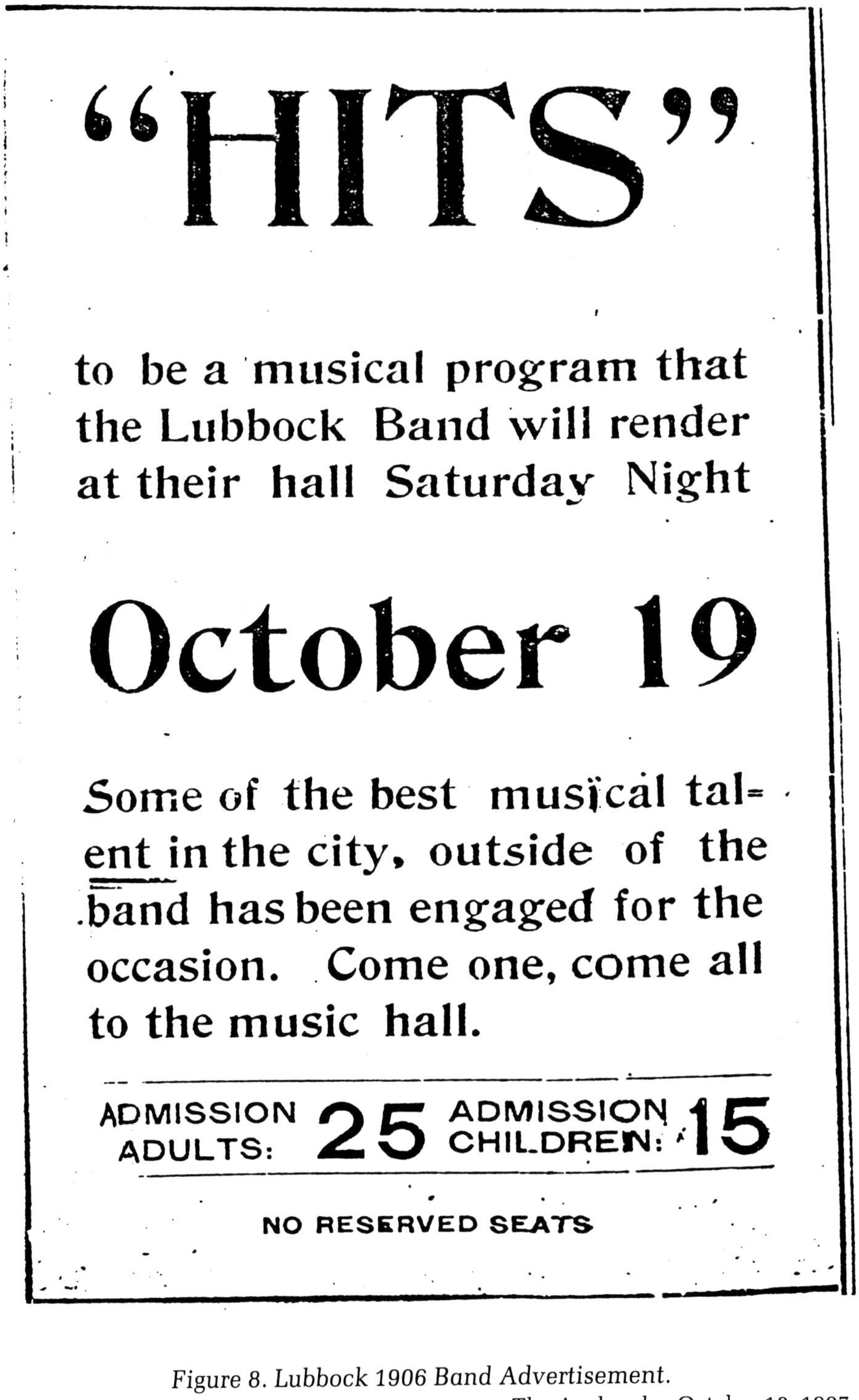

"HITS"

to be a musical program that the Lubbock Band will render at their hall Saturday Night

October 19

Some of the best musical talent in the city, outside of the band has been engaged for the occasion. Come one, come all to the music hall.

ADMISSION ADULTS: **25**   ADMISSION CHILDREN: **15**

NO RESERVED SEATS

Figure 8. Lubbock 1906 Band Advertisement.
— *The Avalanche, October 18, 1907, p. 6.*

PROGRAM

Of The Lubbock Band Concert, Thursday Night,
November 14th.

1. Quickstep "Welcome"   -   -   Band

2. March "Donator"   -   -   -   Band

3. Duett, Cornet and Trombone   -   Carlock and Wilson

4. March "Return of the 47th Regiment"   -   Band

5. Overture "Ladies' Band"   -   -   Band

6. Piano Music

7. Old Plantation Minstrel   -   Five Comedians

8. Piano Music

9. One Act Farce, "Cato, Leb and Col. Spruceup."

Figure 9. Lubbock 1906 Band Program.
— *The Avalanche*, November 8, 1907, p. 8.

In spite of these many positive events — redecorating the Band Hall, a donation from Miss Patterson, rental of the Hall for another year, election of officers for 1908, and a whopping $123.40 recently taken in at the box office — the Lubbock 1906 Band was about to pass from the cultural scene. It made only two further appearances, both in February.[32]

One may never really know what happened to the Lubbock 1906 Band, but its demise can probably be traced to one or several of the following factors. First, the band needed about $70 per month to meet expenses. Unfortunately, the band could not give a concert every month. Time was needed to prepare each program, and the normal rehearsal schedule seems to have been one night a week. Hence, more than $70 had to be taken in at every concert. Making that difficult was the financial hard times that had befallen the town. In numerous notices in the paper throughout the fall of 1907 and the spring of 1908, the merchants called in outstanding debt and advised customers that all further sales would be for cash. Generating high receipts in the throes of hard times may have been impossible.

Second, the plays put on by the band seem to have inspired Lubbock's thespians to form a separate drama group, the Hawthorne Dramatic Club, which was organized in January 1908 and which, through competition for the entertainment dollar, or perhaps quarter, may have contributed to the demise of the band.[33] It is reasonable to suppose that the Club's productions were on a high artistic plane. The community may have felt obligated to give it generous support because all proceeds were donated to civic causes, such as the establishment of a fire department, toward which the Club's first profits went.

Third, other forms of entertainment and other musical activities may have been a factor. As long as cultural opportunity was rather limited, the band could hold its own; but that situation began to change in 1908. In addition to the Hawthorne Dramatic Club, the February 7 *Avalanche* announced a recital by Miss Nancy Patterson's music class "assisted by the Lubbock Orchestra." Another of the town's music teachers, Miss Lula Campbell, also formed an orchestra, and these two orchestras performed frequently during 1908 and beyond.[34] Other music teachers and performers — including Professor Philip Baer, a first-class opera singer — gave concerts. And then came the moving picture, making its Lubbock debut in August 1907.[35] By August 1909, the Orpheum Opera House was showing movies every night.[36]

The greatest problem, however, may been personnel. Four key losses between September 1907 and February 1908 are known,[37] and in

July 1908 a critical loss came with the departure of Ed Carlock, the band teacher.[38] It is difficult to imagine the band carrying on without a replacement; yet if one appeared *The Avalanche* made no mention of it. Moreover, others of the band may have left Lubbock too, for the next band, formed in December 1909, included only seven members from the Lubbock 1906 Band.[39]

To summarize and conclude, the band movement in America found life in Lubbock initially via three bands: the original one formed by Smylie Wilson in late 1904 or early 1905 and disbanded by July 1905, the Lubbock 1906 Band formed some time during that year and lasting at least through February 1908, and a third band formed in December 1909, but which lasted only three or four months (see below, p. 52). Civic pride, personal fulfillment, and the satisfation derived from contributing to the social and cultural welfare of others combined to bring men together three times in Lubbock's early history to form a band. Without question the citizens responded favorably, to judge from attendance records. Earnings, reported by *The Avalanche* for three concerts of the Lubbock 1906 Band, indicate that up to forty percent of the population attended.[40]

The Lubbock 1906 Band's importance to the development of the town, in terms of its role as cultural/entertainment resource for an isolated community as well as its value as town booster to the outside world, cannot be questioned. Unfortunately, a band is very expensive to maintain. The Lubbock 1906 Band depended for revenues primarily on ticket sales, and in a small community gate receipts alone are not likely to sustain a band. What was needed was a chamber of commerce to get behind it, but Lubbock did not yet have one. However, by 1912 a much larger Lubbock built a bandstand in front of the courthouse and a new band, with stronger sources of support, was entertaining the community; but that is the next chapter in the history of Lubbock's bands.

CHAPTER 5

The Municipal Bands, Part II: The Lubbock Band And The Lubbock Cowboy Band

If the three initial efforts to provide the emerging city with a band were short-lived, the main problem was money. There was never enough for instruments, music, uniforms, the hiring of a hall and other concert expenses, and, above all, to attract and retain a competent band teacher. Most of the players were beginners; without a teacher, they could make little if any progress. A case in point was the Lubbock Concert Band, formed in December 1909. This band did not survive long enough to give even a single public concert, for its director/teacher, S. W. Pease, left Lubbock in March 1910 for a trip to Mexico, where he then remained.[1] Without a director/teacher, the organization quickly dissolved.

THE LUBBOCK BAND

The previous chapter concluded with the suggestion that a municipal band was necessarily an expensive proposition, probably more than a city of about 1,000 residents could maintain. A larger Lubbock might enjoy better success. Let us consider whether it did.

During 1910, 1911, and the beginning of 1912, Lubbock was entirely without a civic band. The large advertisement in the newspaper for the July 4 celebration of 1911 lists an extensive program of events, everything from a Baby Show and a Sack Race to a Potato Race and a Base Ball Game — but no mention of a band concert.[2] The old bandwagon of the Lubbock 1906 Band was used to lead the merchants' parade, and inside was indeed a band — not Lubbock's but that of the visiting Mollie Bailey Circus.[3]

Around the beginning of 1912, the city directory put the population at a vastly increased 3,500.[4] And the newspaper proposed that Lubbock try again to organize and support a band. An editorial lamented "Don't know, we may be wrong, but it seems that Lubbock is mighty quiet without a brass band. Why not re-organize and make the old town ring with the music thereof."[5] And again that winter: "We have occasionally heard it said that we need a brass band and we rather think, yes."[6]

Such seeds, planted firmly and nurtured gently by Editor Dow, finally produced results in the spring; on May 9, the paper announced that "A move is on foot now to organize a brass band in Lubbock." The key ingredient, a director/teacher, had been found: "Prof. N. C. Bishop formerly of the Canyon City Band is in our city and is talking the matter up among the band men of town." And the editor believed sufficient funding to undertake the enterprise might be forthcoming: "All the business men have not been interviewed but those who have been approached on the subject are highly in favor of the organization and will pledge a liberal support." Professor Bishop submitted a proposal for funding, and the paper predicted that it would be accepted at an upcoming meeting of representative businessmen. The paper further added that if the proposal were accepted, Lubbock would be the only town on the South Plains to have a band, the significance of which would be a great victory over every other South Plains community.[7]

With Lubbock competing for leadership with numerous other South Plains towns, the prestige, booster, and cultural value of a band could not be emphasized too highly. Hence, hardly an issue of the newspaper appeared without some reference to the enterprise, as Editor James L. Dow, Lubbock booster extraordinaire, threw the full weight of his office behind the project.

Dow's powerful, sustained effort would not go unrewarded. Not only did the business and professional men provide funding sufficient to launch the band, but the county stepped in behind the organization, building a bandstand on the lawn in front of the courthouse for "weekly" band concerts.[8] Soon, Dow's enterprise was ready to offer the first public concert of music by a Lubbock band in over four years.

The Lubbock Band, as it came to be known, made its public debut on June 29, 1912, on a program for the benefit of the local Fire Department.[9] With the completion of the bandstand by July 4, the stage was set for regular summer band concerts.[10] The newspaper then reported three more concerts in quick succession: on July 26 at the bandstand; on August 2 for an out-of-town engagement at Gomez, Texas, for which the band was well paid; and on August 8, again at the bandstand. On October 11, the Lubbock Band presented at the Opera House a four-act play entitled "Uncle Josh." The event was billed as a fund-raiser for the band, and again the newspaper threw its full weight behind the project. It printed spot announcements on many pages of the October 3 issue, a large advertisement in the October 10 issue including a synopsis of each act and a complete cast listing, a page one review in the October 17 issue, informing the readership of, among other things, gate receipts over $100, and a notice in the October 24 issue that the band is taking the play on the road, to Crosbyton, Texas. On November 15, the band put on another play at the Opera House, "The Face at the Window," and again the newspaper, by way of encouraging attendance, provided a synopsis of each act plus the full cast.

Despite support from the newspaper and apparently from the citizens as well, the Lubbock Band immediately passed from the pages of the town's history. The group's fate is unknown, but by May 1913 it had been replaced by the Lubbock Cowboy Band under the direction not of N. C. Bishop but of Monte Bowron.

One clue to the demise of the Lubbock Band is the absence of musical performances by the band after August 8. Most likely, director Bishop left Lubbock during August 1912 or shortly thereafter. Without a director/teacher to hold the band together musically, the men turned to plays, the old-timers in the group undoubtedly remembering the success of the plays put on by the Lubbock 1906 Band.[11] All known performances by the Lubbock Band are listed in Appendix C.

THE LUBBOCK COWBOY BAND

The first available reference to the Lubbock Cowboy Band appeared in the May 8, 1913 issue of *The Lubbock Avalanche*, but the band had been formed earlier. Monte Bowron, its director, was in Lubbock on "business" in October 1912 and again in November.[12] He may well have been negotiating for the then-vacant position of municipal band director. The date of his move from Snyder to Lubbock is unknown; but the astonishingly strong condition of the band by May suggests a reformulation of the Lubbock Band perhaps as early as January 1913.

The name "Lubbock Cowboy Band" was more than appropriate for a West Texas band, it was descriptive too. The band actually dressed in cowboy fashion, with "leggins, spurs, and full cowboy regalia."[13] The idea most likely originated with the new band director, Monte Bowron, who must have thought that some kind of outfit was called for, accepting cowboy dress in the absence of funds for band uniforms. Fund-raising efforts in May and June 1913 did result in the purchase of uniforms, first worn for an engagement in Shallowater, Texas on June 26, 1913 (shown in Plate 6). The suits were of dark blue, trimmed in black; the caps were of the same material, but trimmed in gold.[14] Name recognition, however, had become so great that although the dress changed, the name did not. And so "Lubbock Cowboy Band" was no longer descriptive, only appropriate.

Incidentally, Lubbock's unofficial poet laureate, George M. Hunt, contributed to the uniform fund-raising effort, bestowing a singular honor upon the band at the First Monday Trades Day dinner on May 5, 1913. The proceeds of the dinner that day, $112, were dedicated to the band uniform fund. During dinner, a quartet sang an arrangement of "Dixie" to a poem by Hunt, entitled "Our Cow Boy Band," the full text of which is given in Figure 10.[15] The words fit well enough, the sentiment is appropriate, and one can imagine the band's pleasure at the result: immortalized in poetry and $112 in the bank to boot!

Monte Bowron must have been an outstanding teacher and director, for by May 1913, the praises of the band were being sung far and wide, even though Bowron had been director only a few months. The commendations came in connection with the 1913 Reunion of the United Confederate Veterans, May 27–29, in Chattanooga, Tennessee. Over 100,000 visitors were expected, including Captain Barr's Confederate Grays of Fort Worth, who requested C. F. Woods, Western Passenger Agent for the Texas and Pacific and Queen and Crescent Railroad, to invite the Lubbock Cowboy Band to accompany them. Realizing that the band would need an official invitation from the committee planning musical events at the reunion, Woods sent the following letter to the District Passenger Agent at Chattanooga:

> Will you please use your influence with the Music Committee at Chattanooga with reference to securing an engagement for the Lubbock Cowboy Band, Lubbock, Texas, during the confederate reunion at Chattanooga.
>
> I don't believe that your committee fully realizes what this band would mean to them. It is a real cowboy band, and the only one in Texas. They dress in cowboy style, wear leggins, spurs and full cowboy

OUR COW BOY BAND.

To tune--Dixie

COMPOSED BY GEO. M. HUNT.

Sang by Quartette in Dining Hall First Monday, May 5th.

1.

Our Cow Boy Band is something great,
The very best one in the state.
Hurrah! Hurrah! Hurrah! for our Cow Boy Band.
Come brothers all and sisters to
And welcome them with honor due.
Hurrah! Hurrah! Hurrah! for our Cow Boy Band.

Chorus.

Our Cow Boy Band's a dandy,
Hurrah! Hurrah!
They always come in handy,
Yes, they always come in handy.
Hurrah! Hurrah!
They always come in handy.

2.

With hammer and saw they went to work,
And made these tables and none did shirk,
Hurrah Hurrah! Hurrah! for our Cow Boy Band.
When e're we've anything to do
They sail right in and help us thru
Hurrah! Hurrah! Hurrah! for our Cow Boy Band.

Chorus.

3.

Let's all keep on and give them aid,
And we will surely feel repaid,
Hurrah! Hurrah! Hurrah! for our Cow Boy Band.
They play for this and they play for that,
And never say "Please pass the hat."
Hurrah! Hurrah! Hurrah! for our Cow Boy Band.

Chorus.

Figure 10. Poem "Our Cow Boy Band" by George M. Hunt.
— The Lubbock Avalanche, May 8, 1913, p. 6

regalia. In addition to this, it is one of the best bands in Texas. They received a great deal of notice and favorable comment at Macon.

I wish that you would please see what you can do in regard to this matter at your earliest convenience and advise.[16]

The performance at Macon (perhaps Macon, Georgia, or Macon, Texas, a small village in Franklin County in the northeast part of the state) must have taken place before May 1, 1913 and is, aside from this notice, undocumented. Nevertheless, it was sufficient to earn the band "a great deal of notice and favorable comment," as well as the considerable effort of Mr. Woods to thrust the band into the national spotlight.

In the end, however, the reunion took place without the Lubbock Cowboy Band. Perhaps the planning committees had already completed arrangements by the time Woods' letter to Chattanooga, written after all only a few weeks before the event, arrived. Whatever the case, Editor Dow, never missing an opportunity to boost his band or point out its contribution to the community, must have soothed the disappointment somewhat with these kind words:

> The Lubbock Band is becoming one of the greatest advertising mediums that Lubbock has and is worthy of every cent that is expended to keep it going.
>
> People abroad are speaking of Lubbock as having an up-to-date band and know that the town is worth while, as it is only good towns that will maintain a musical organization such as the Lubbock Cowboy Band is.
>
> This organization is doing a great deal in the way of advertising the town, and the results will soon begin to be felt. A few, not many, seem to think that the expenditure of a dollar each month to maintain the band is money thrown away, but to those who have that idea, we would suggest that they dismiss such from their mind, for we believe it is money well spent.[17]

The disappointment of Chattanooga notwithstanding, numerous other performances did materialize during the spring and summer of 1913. It seemed that no large outdoor gathering that summer was complete without band music. The period proved so busy for the band that we may well consider the highlights of its activity.

After Macon, the next known performance of the Lubbock Cowboy Band was on May 5, 1913, at the First Monday Trades Day. One of the great cooperative efforts of the city, the Trades Days became an ongoing monthly event beginning in February or March 1913.[18] On the first Monday of each month, the merchants held a big sale to attract to the city customers from the entire region. The Lubbock Retail Merchants' Association and, probably later, the Lubbock Chamber of Commerce provided support and organization. Drawings for free merchandise sweetened the inducement to visitors, and a large crowd could always be expected. These Trades Day sales were highly successful and continued at least until the summer of 1914. The half-page advertisement for the Monday, June 3, 1913 Trades Day (Figure 11) shows typical activities and the prominent position in those activities occupied by the band.[19]

On May 23 the band gave what may have been its first outdoor, evening concert of the summer season. The program, thoughtfully printed in the newspaper for the edification of the citizens, happens to be the only program available for this band:

March "Glorification"	Rosenkrans
Overture "Bouquet"	Laurendeau
March "Colonel Miners"	Rosenkrans
Waltzes "Flowers of the Wild Woods"	Skaggs
Sacred March "Adoration"	Miller
Overture "Sincerity"	Barnard
Serenade "Fond Hearts"	Rathburn
Overture "Impromptu"	Dalbey[20]

The program is typical of good American municipal bands of the time — marches, waltzes, overtures, and popular songs — and it points to a band of no mean ability. Moreover, there was about one hour of music. The Lubbock 1906 Band, it will be recalled, was never strong enough to undertake a complete program; solo and ensemble numbers and often a short play rounded out the program (see above, p.). The Lubbock Cowboy Band, with its professional director, was more than capable of meeting the challenge. Moreover, there is no evidence that the numerous concerts of this band ever included anything but band selections.

Beginning June 19, 1913, Lubbockites were invited to attend band concerts every Thursday evening through the summer months. The concerts were free; the programs, popular. Ever larger crowds attended, prompting the editor of the paper, by August, to comment, "There is quite an increasing interest in these weekly affairs and it is a foregone conclusion that the people are beginning to properly appreciate the band." Moreover, he added, the band's reputation had grown to the point where it was invited to play more out-of-town engagements that summer than any other band on the South Plains.[21]

The most significant of those took place at Shallowater, Texas on

First Monday Trades Day
LUBBOCK, JUNE 2nd.

Our regular monthly Trades Day event is close at hand again. You know the success of our previous dates, and we assure you that in no respect will the FIRST MONDAY IN JUNE be less interesting and profitable to you. We appreciate your presence in the city on these occasions, and extend a cordial invitation to come to Lubbock next Monday.

FORTY DOLLARS IN PREMIUMS TO BE GIVEN AWAY

A considerable list of premiums have been offered by the different firms which will go to our country friends and patrons—and ask that you read the following list and the proposition that is submitted to you below:

Each person 18 years of age and over, who resides outside of the incorporation limits of the city of Lubbock, are requested to register their name in a book that will be kept for that purpose. The name will be written opposite a number and the one registering will be given a number corresponding to it, and its corresponding number will at the same time be placed in a box. At four o'clock the numbers will be shaken up, and a disinterested party will draw from that box one number, and the party holding a like number will be entitled to the first premium, and so on down the line till the number of premiums are taken up. Don't forget to register. The book will be located at the northwest corner of the Lubbock Mercantile Building and a man will have charge of it and will give you additional information if desired. The premiums offered are absolutely free, and are to be paid in merchandise out of the store at which they are offered:

The Lubbock Mercantile Co., merchandise $5.00.	I. B. Wright, knife $2.00	W. A. Brown & Co., dry goods $1.50.
Shelby Dry Goods Co., merchandise $3.00.	W. E. Robinson, merchandise $2.00.	City Meat Market, 10 pounds lard $1.50.
O'Neal & Penney, choice of hat or corset $5.00.	Lubbock Drug Co., merchandise $2.00.	Hunt Grocery Co., 3 lb can Manor House Coffee $1.20.
Jno. P. Lewis & Co., merchandise $2.50.	Martin & Wolcott, sack of White Crest Flour $1.75.	W. S. Clark, 1 dozen cans corn $1.00.
R. A. Rankin & Sons, aluminum double boiler $2.50.	B. P. Hopkins, merchandise $1.50.	Adams Grocery Company, Cheek-Neal coffee $1.00.
Western Windmill Co., merchandise $2.50.	Long Bros., 25 pounds granulated sugar $1.50.	Avalanche Publishing Co., year's subscription $1.00.
Red Cross Drug Co., merchandise $2.50.	Cash Meat Market, 10 pounds lard $1.50.	

Trading All Day: bring your trading stock.	Band Concert from 2:00 o'clock to 3 o'clock in the afternoon.
The Lubbock Cowboy Band will furnish music.	Awarding of premiums at 4 o'clock.
Dinner will be served as usual at 12 o'clock at the Opera House.	Bring your poultry. We have a place to exhibit them.

Lubbock's Trade Day is not an experiment. It has been tried and found most satisfactory to everyone concerned. Others follow but Lubbock remains in the lead, and our merchants are prepared to take care of your needs in all lines of merchandise.

COME MAKE THE FIRST MONDAY IN JUNE THE BEST ONE YET.

RETAIL MERCHANT'S ASSOCIATION

Figure 11. Trades Day Advertisement.

— *The Lubbock Avalanche*, May 29, 1913, p. 3

June 26 and at Littlefield, Texas on July 4. In both cases Lubbock's band was part of a grand celebration; fortunately, many of the details have been preserved.

As the Santa Fe connection from Lubbock through Shallowater to Texico (and on to the West Coast) neared completion, the former Ripley Townsite, with the new name of Shallowater, prepared to take its place on the map. A huge celebration was planned and announced by a notice, no doubt appearing in many newspapers, inviting all to come (Figure 12).[22]

Arranged for this special occasion was a train from Lubbock, the first ever to Shallowater, that part of the line from Lubbock to Texico recently completed. The program for the day, with its attention to detail and its wide variety of excellent events, would guarantee that a good time was had by all:

[1.] After the crowd had assembled under the arbor, which had been built especially for the occasion, all were entertained by a few choice selections from the band.

[2.] About 11:00 A.M. the people were ushered into the school house, where they listened to the literary program. First came a hearty welcome to all from Bro. Word followed by response from Judge McGee of Lubbock. Then Shallowater's boys and girls displayed their talents, and they do indeed deserve praise. The program though brief was well rendered.

[3.] While the band boys were playing some appropriate selections, the good ladies of Shallowater were spreading the dinner and after everything was in readiness and dinner announced, all, with quickened step and smiling faces, assembled at the tables and the spread was one of the finest that it has ever been my pleasure to enjoy. Barbecued meats, bread, pickles, choice cakes, pies, salads and coffee constituted this delicious report [repast?].

[4.] At 2:30 P.M. the band began to play; the crowd soon re-assembled and were [next] entertained by the singers of Shallowater, Lubbock and other places.

[5.] Some time was spent in the sale of lots and several choice business lots were sold.

[6.] Bronco riding and tournament racing were the entertaining features for the remainder of the day . . . The band furnished music during [the] games.

[7.] At 5:30 P.M. another spread was made and lunch served to all who desired to partake . . .[23]

As impressive as the celebration at Shallowater was, the one at Littlefield matched if not exceeded it. Events were set in motion on June 7, 1912, when Major George Washington Littlefield signed a contract with

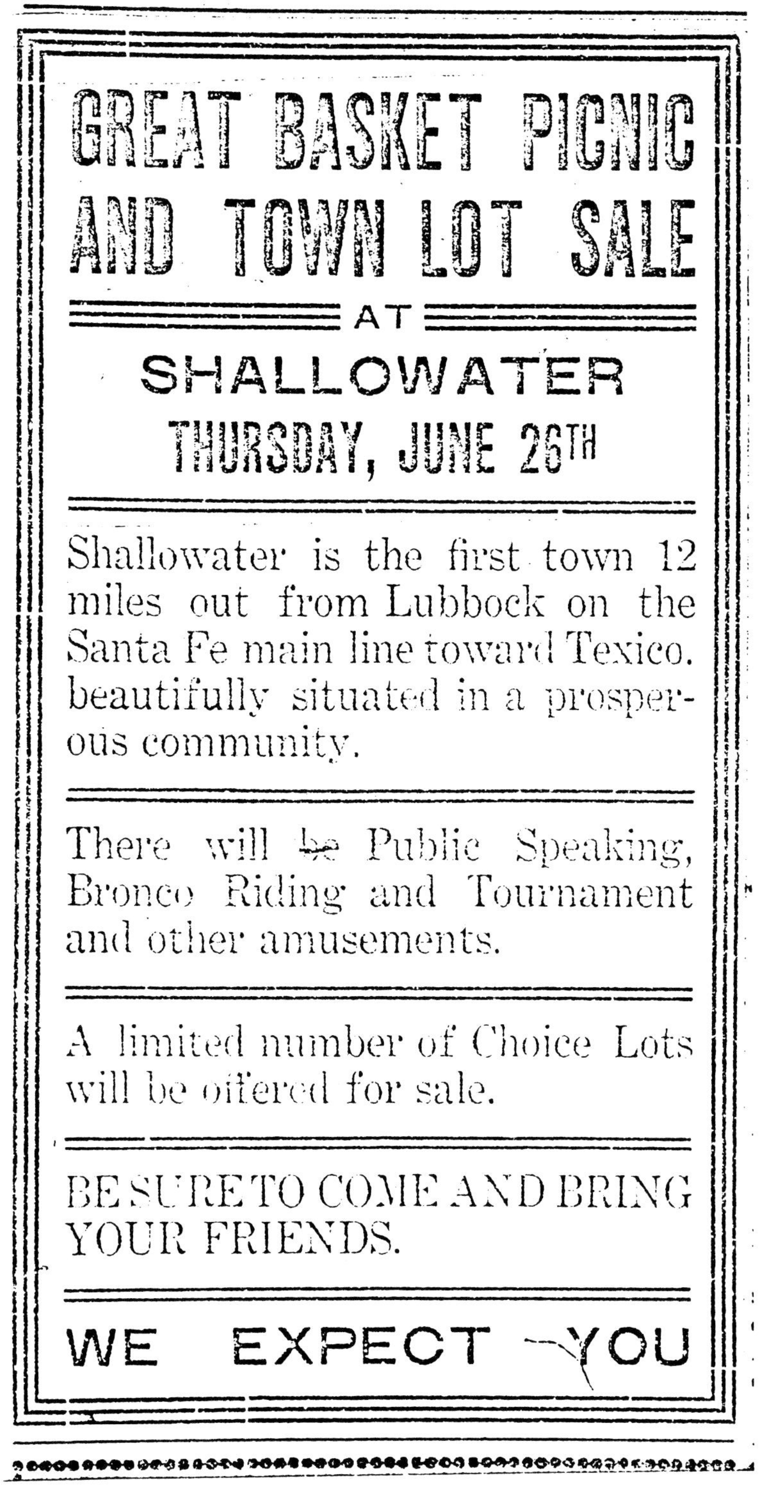

GREAT BASKET PICNIC
AND TOWN LOT SALE
AT
SHALLOWATER
THURSDAY, JUNE 26TH

Shallowater is the first town 12 miles out from Lubbock on the Santa Fe main line toward Texico. beautifully situated in a prosperous community.

There will be Public Speaking, Bronco Riding and Tournament and other amusements.

A limited number of Choice Lots will be offered for sale.

BE SURE TO COME AND BRING YOUR FRIENDS.

WE   EXPECT   YOU

Figure 12. Advertisement for Shallowater, Texas.
— *The Lubbock Avalanche,* June 12, 1913, p. 9

the Santa Fe Railroad to extend the Lubbock-Texico line through his Yellow House Ranch, covering about 300,000 acres in Hockley, Lamb, Bailey, and Cochran counties of West Texas. He then created the Littlefield Lands Company to market the property and founded the town bearing his name. Once a hotel large enough to accommodate the great number of expected visitors was completed (Casa Amarillo Hotel, March 5–6) Major Littlefield and his sales manager A. P. Duggan set about selecting an appropriate date for the official opening of the town. They agreed on the Fourth of July, 1913, and developed plans for a massive celebration. About 1,400 persons gathered to watch the official opening, coming to Littlefield on foot, on horseback, in wagons, or on the special train from Lubbock. A. P. Duggan's program for the day included an enormous meal at noon consisting of barbecued beef, beans, and other chuck-wagon dishes served in "regular cowboy style," a guest speaker (the state commissioner of agriculture), a baseball game between Lubbock and Richland, N.M., horse races, various side shows, and a gala dance in the evening. Duggan also promised that "the West Texas ranch life will be given full sway, and the cowboys of Yellow House Ranch and adjoining ranches will have the pleasure of demonstrating to the visitors the 'how' of the genuine round-up of 2,000 head of range cattle, making use of the branding iron, together with a realistic bronc busting exhibition."[24] And to serenade the guests, he hired the Lubbock Cowboy Band, which again played several times during the day. Clearly, Lubbock's new band was off to a galloping start worthy of its name.

In addition to gate receipts and fees for out-of-town engagements, financial support must also have come from the businessmen of town, probably from the Lubbock Chamber of Commerce, formed in 1913. Surely the role the band could play in helping the city reach its goals was not lost on the Chamber of Commerce, at least not while Editor Dow was in office. Conversely, the band could not have continued to function — and this one did for some time — without financial support from the business community. Nevertheless, since no Chamber records prior to 1916 exist, one finds only indirect evidence. The Chamber's support most likely took the form of a salary paid directly to the band director; this was a common practice. The salary together with earnings from music lessons to the bandsmen were probably what induced Monte Bowron to Lubbock.[25]

Financial support also came from an unexpected quarter: that generous and compassionate manager of the Opera House and the Lyric Theatre, E. M. McElroy. He came to the band's assistance by dedicating to it one-half the proceeds of certain showings at the Lyric.[26] The band boys, printing a grateful response to his first band benefit, explained the arrangement:

> Through the kindness of the editor, we take this method of thanking the manager of the Lyric Theater for courtesies extended the band . . . We appreciate those who did attend and wish to make the following announcement for the future: the Lyric Theater will give a Band Benefit show on the second Tuesday in each month. We kindly ask the people to remember this, and assist the band by attending the benefit shows . . .
> Yours, for a permanent band for Lubbock —
> Lubbock Cowboy Band[27]

With the arrival of summer, 1914, the cycle of open-air concerts at the bandstand resumed: Friday evenings, eight o'clock. The band intended to continue the weekly concerts throughout the summer, but whether it did, and how extensive and successful its other activities were, is unknown. At this point, the principal witness to the band's activities becomes mute; issues of *The Lubbock Avalanche* from July 9, 1914 through August 22, 1918 are, with few exceptions, unavailable.[28] Hence, after July 4, 1914, only two further performances by the band are documented. A list of all known performances of the Lubbock Cowboy Band is offered in Appendix C.

MEMBERSHIP

Discussed earlier in this chapter were two major out-of-town engagements of the band in 1913: on June 26 at a celebration in Shallowater and on July 4 at the formal opening of the town of Littlefield. Fortunately, photographers recorded the band's presence on those two occasions (Plates 5–7).

The picture shown in Plate 5 was in the possession of Katie Bell Crump, daughter of pioneer W. D. Crump. The upper left-hand corner is inscribed, "Celebrating R.R.," and across the bottom is written, "Picnic at Shallowater Tex June 26, 1913." A rather large group of people is on hand, including, in the center of the picture, the Lubbock Cowboy Band. Fifteen bandsmen appear in Plate 5, but the photograph was taken at almost too great a distance to be useful for identification of the men. The Texas Tech Museum contains another photograph of a band resplendent and dignified in their high-neck uniforms. Although of excellent quality, the picture lacks description or identification (Plate 6).[29] Comparison of

Plate 5. The Lubbock Cowboy Band, 1913.
— Photo courtesy Katie Bell Crump, Lubbock, Texas

[64]

Plate 6. The Lubbock Cowboy Band, 1913.
— Photo courtesy Museum, Texas Tech University,
Lubbock, Texas

[65]

Plate 7. The Lubbock Cowboy Band, 1913.
— Photo courtesy Southwest Collection, Texas Tech
University, Lubbock, Texas

the two under magnification not only reveals the same bandsmen, but also permits with some certainty the conclusion that the building in the background is the same in each.[30] It is highly probable that both were taken at Shallowater on June 26, 1913. Significantly, in Plate 6 the face of every bandsman can be seen clearly, permitting identification of the men.

Another excellent photograph (Plate 7) was located in the Texas Tech University Southwest Collection;[31] on the back is written (by an anonymous hand) "Littlefield Lands Co — Lubbock Band on Opening Day July 4, 1913." A chart comparing the membership of Plates 6 and 7, based on facial and instrument comparison, is given in Figure 13.[32]

The photographs do not, however, by themselves reveal the identification of the bandsmen. Only six are certain (Plate 6):

> Monte Bowron, middle row, 2nd from left
> Frank Lester, middle row, 2nd from right
> James W. Partin, middle row, far right
> Al Rankin, middle row, 3rd from right
> Will Ross, bottom row, 2nd from right
> Smylie Wilson, top row, 2nd from left

Dolly (Mrs. Robert) Bowron identified her father-in-law and provided much helpful information about him.[33] Born in Kansas on October 26, 1876, Monte Bowron played a significant role, spanning almost a decade, in the history of Lubbock's bands. Prior to Lubbock, he had directed the municipal band at Snyder, Texas, at least since 1907 and perhaps since the turn of the century. In 1913, at age thirty-six, he came to Lubbock, most likely at the invitation of the city to re-organize the now defunct Lubbock Band into the Lubbock Cowboy Band. After World War I, yet another band was formed with Bowron at its head, the Lubbock Chamber of Commerce Band, which lasted until May 1922. Afterwards, Bowron took over direction of the band at Lorenzo, and over the years numerous other bands were added to his list of directorships, among them those at Post, Tahoka, Brownfield, Littlefield, Southland, Crosbyton, Ralls and Petersburg.[34]

Bowron came from a musical family; his two older brothers were bandsmen, his sister was an organist. He began playing instruments when he was six years old, and by age seventeen was a band director. Bowron was capable not only of leading the band through successful concerts, but also of teaching all the men in the band who were in need of instruction — and that was most of them. He evidently could play all wind instruments. Lubbock was fortunate to have the services of such a

FIGURE 13

Plate 6	Plate 7	Instrument	Identification
Top row 1*	Third row 4*	Bass drum	
Top row 2	Top row 5	Slide trombone	S. C. Wilson
Top row 3	Third row 1	Flugelhorn	
Middle row 1	Second row 2?	Cornet	
Middle row 2	Bottom row 1	Cornet	Monte Bowron
Middle row 3	Second row 3	Cornet	
Middle row 4	Third row 2	Alto horn	
Middle row 5	Top row 3	Helicon	Al Rankin
Middle row 6	Second row 4?	Cornet	Frank Lester
Middle row 7	Top row 1	Valve trombone	J. W. Partin
Bottom row 1	Top row 2	Baritone horn	
Bottom row 2	Absent	E♭ Clarinet	
Bottom row 3	Bottom row 2	B♭ Clarinet	
Bottom row 4	Top row 4	Baritone horn	Will Ross
Bottom row 5	Second row 1	Snare drum	
	Third row 3	Alto horn	
	Second row 5	Cornet	
	Second row 6	Baritone horn	

* Numbering is from left to right

distinguished professional for about nine years. He provided welcome stability to both bandsmen and community while serving as permanent director/teacher. And with the Chamber of Commerce providing a salary,[35] it was to Bowron's benefit to make Lubbock his home, which he did from 1913 to 1922 and again from about 1940 until his death in 1956.

The Rev. James W. Partin personally identified himself and his close friends Frank Lester and Al Rankin.[36] Rev. Partin was born in 1896; the family moved to Lubbock in 1907, and then left in 1914, not to return. He played in the band in 1913 and 1914 and, among other things, remembered numerous out-of-town engagements in Littlefield, Hereford, Tahoka, Brownfield, and Plainview. He confirmed that Monte Bowron taught all the men in the band who needed instruction, including Partin on the trombone.[37]

Two other bandsmen, who were in Lubbock's earlier bands and whose absence from this band would have been unlikely, were Will Ross and Smylie Wilson. Both were identified by relatives.[38] It will be recalled that Smylie Wilson organized Lubbock's first band in 1904 or 1905 and that he and Will Ross were faithful members of all Lubbock's early bands.

THE DEMISE OF THE BAND

Lawrence Graves suggested that the Lubbock Cowboy Band ended in 1914, "because after 1914 no more was heard from it."[39] However, it was not the band that ceased after 1914, but available issues of the newspaper, the principal witness to its activities. Another witness, Myrtie Agnew, claims the band was going strong in 1915 and perhaps through 1916.[40] Born in 1898, she came to Lubbock in 1910 and in September 1914 married Hoyt Agnew. She recalled that her husband joined the band after their marriage and that she accompanied him to rehearsals and concerts until the birth of their first child, on February 16, 1916. She particularly remembered going with the band to the Fourth of July celebration in Brownfield in 1915. She is certain of the year because it was the Fourth of July after her marriage but before the birth of her child. Mrs. Raymond George, at that same celebration in Brownfield, confirmed the year; it was her first in this area of West Texas.[41] Finally, one of only two available issues of *The Lubbock Avalanche* for 1916 attests to the band's continuation at least until September 13, 1916, on which day it played for a visiting delegation from Abilene.[42]

The significance of such discoveries is that they extend the life of the band more than two years, making it Lubbock's most successful and long-lived band yet, and proving not only that the community was willing to support a "permanent" band, but also that the band had become part of the cultural identity of the community.

While Mrs. Agnew did not recall precisely when or under what circumstances the band disbanded, an educated guess might be offered. The Lubbock Cowboy Band, which commenced music-making in early 1913, was still going strong in the fall of 1916. One expects it would have continued many more years had not World War I intervened, bringing financial hard times to the region and carrying off to battle men from the band. A band based on such a romantic notion as the cowboy deserves an appropriately romantic denouement: an heroic end in the service of its country.

CHAPTER 6

Other Cultural Resources: Music Teachers, Local Theater, Local Orchestras, and Public School Music

MUSIC TEACHERS

According to Margaret Huff, who settled in Lubbock in 1912 and subsequently became one of the most influential music educators in the city's history, Philip E. Baer was probably the most colorful musician and teacher on the Lubbock scene around 1910. Educated in Milan, Italy, for a career in opera, he was said to have had a voice so much like the great Caruso's that one could scarcely distinguish between them. Baer's career as an operatic tenor, however, was cut short by paralysis; crippled, he was forced to trade the stage for the studio.[1]

His first visit to Lubbock appears to have occurred in September 1907 when, assisted by his music class from Hale Center, Texas, he presented a voice recital in the Band Hall for the benefit of the Lubbock Library Association. The students performed numerous selections; the professor sang four solos and gave a lecture as well. The newspaper's review pronounced the program "splendid" and the audience "intelligent and appreciative," and ended with the hope that this would not be the professor's last visit.[2] It wasn't. Baer returned in the summer of 1908 to teach a class in Lubbock. The summer's efforts culminated in a concert of Grand Opera on August 28, repeated on August 29. It was a first for the town, as the newspaper admitted: "Hearing grand opera sung is a treat never as yet enjoyed by this part of Texas."[3] The treat consisted of arias from Gounod's *Faust,* Donizetti's *Lucia di Lammermoor,* and Verdi's *Il Trovatore* and *Aida* — repertoire difficult and challenging by any measure. Professor Baer must have been a teacher of considerable ability, who found in Lubbock students of considerable talent or at least zeal.

The concert concluded, Baer headed east for the winter, as before. If he returned the following summer, the paper made no mention of it. His activities were next chronicled in the spring of 1910, when he arranged a music class for that summer, which would turn out to be his last in Lubbock.[4] During this stay he gave two solo recitals, and the music class once again came to an end with a concert of Grand Opera. In a four-column review, the editor referred to the event as "a decidedly classy musical recital."[5] The program featured vocal solos, duets, trios, quartets, and even one quintet. Highlights included a ballad entitled "Waiting" sung by Mrs. Van Sanders, who displayed "a voice of much sweetness and expression;" Verdi's "Hear Us Oh Lord," sung by Mrs. Frank Wheelock, soprano, Smylie Wilson, bass, and Professor Baer, tenor, which "elicited no little applause;" and Mrs. Oscar Tubbs' rendition of "The Lost Chord." Also delighting the audience was Bonnie Hudgins' performance of the "Flower Song" from Gounod's *Faust,* which "was awarded unstinted applause." But according to the reviewer, Mrs. William Claxton singing the "Jewel Song" from *Faust* was a showstopper "of particular high order . . . sung from start to finish without a false note." Clearly, Grand Opera, well performed, was a welcome addition to the town's cultural fare.

Professor Baer's students were adults.[6] The needs of the young members of the community were met largely by two other music teachers up until about 1910: Nancy Patterson and Lula Campbell.

Nancy Patterson was a violinist primarily, a pianist and singer secondarily. She came to Lubbock from Temple, Texas, from where, in August 1907, she placed the following brief notice in *The Avalanche:* "I shall be in Lubbock soon to work up an interest in my music class for the coming year."[7] The paper subsequently reported her "return" to Lubbock; most likely, then, she first came to Lubbock the previous school year.[8]

During the 1907–08 school year, the newspaper took note of three recitals by Miss Patterson's music class, on October 12, November 25, and February 7. Such a heavy performance schedule might be taken as evidence of a large, talented, and hard-working class of students. The last recital is of special interest; it included the debut of an orchestra under her direction, about which more later.[9]

Concerned with improvement of her pedagogical skills, she traveled to Chicago in August 1909 to enroll in a one-week music seminar at the Bush Temple Conservatory of Music.[10] On her return, she resumed her music class for the 1909–10 school year. That year also saw her very active not only as teacher and orchestra conductor, but also as solo performer. In the spring of 1910, accompanied by local pianist Hattie McGee, she presented several violin recitals. In either July or October, some confusion exists, she married a wealthy rancher, B. E. Fuller, and shortly thereafter disappeared from musical view, perhaps no longer teaching or, more likely, having moved with her husband away from Lubbock.[11] Through her numerous solo recitals, the regular concerts of her music class, and the performances of her orchestra, Nancy Patterson made an enormous contribution to the musical life of Lubbock during the years 1906–1910.

So too did fellow music teacher Lula Campbell: pianist, teacher of piano, voice, and other instruments, and orchestra conductor as well. As noted in Chapter 1, Lula Campbell had established a music school in Lubbock as early as fall 1905; indeed, she was Lubbock's first professional, resident music teacher. On November 29, 1905, she and her students presented a class recital at the courthouse, perhaps the first of its kind in Lubbock, including about two hours of singing, recitations, and instrumental music.[12] The newspaper did not reveal the size of her class, but it noted elsewhere that a few months earlier, during the summer of 1905, a T. D. Mullins got together a class of thirty-four pupils. Since the population of Lubbock at the time was around 800, thirty-four children represented a significant portion of Lubbock's youth studying music.[13]

Her studio was thriving and its activities frequently made news. It was her practice not to give class recitals in the course of the school year, but rather to present one grand recital at its conclusion: on May 1, 1908, June 4, 1909, and June 24, 1910.[14] The last of these, for example, presented thirty-one pupils in twenty-five individual numbers, from which the newspaper singled out Miss Myrel Adams and Miss Eva Wheelock as exceptional young talents. The paper concluded its review by noting: "And so closed another year of Miss Campbell's teaching in Lubbock. Her ability and success are best attested by the fact that more applications are made for instruction than she can personally give."[15]

By 1910 her reputation was so well established that she was selected one of two teachers of music to teach in the Lubbock High School building for the 1910–11 school year.[16] Ever vigilant about her own educational skills, and perhaps in anticipation of the new assignment, she traveled to Amarillo during the summer of 1910 to take two courses, one in piano and the other in violin.[17]

In the fall of 1912, as she was preparing to re-open her studio in connection with the public school, an apparently last-minute college opening for a teacher of violin and piano enticed her to the Baptist College in Canadian, Texas.[18] She returned to Lubbock after the academic year, but did not re-open her studio in the fall. Her coordination of a musical program in association with a grand display put on by the merchants of the city, in October 1913, may have been her last musical association with Lubbock. In late October, she was off to Florida for a visit that apparently became permanent;[19] perhaps her experience with college teaching had opened up new ambitions to her that Lubbock, without a college, could not satisfy.

Rounding out the list of active private music teachers in Lubbock before 1910 is Willie Cowan. Evidently a most capable pianist, she was selected to play in the Lubbock Orchestra, to accompany Philip Baer in his recitals, and to accompany another voice teacher and singer, J. H. Wiggington, who came to Lubbock for a short time during the summer of 1909.[20] Moreover, along with Lula Campbell, she was appointed to give music lessons at Lubbock High School during the 1910–11 academic year.[21] When Lula Campbell and the recently-arrived Harriet Brown were given the academic appointments for the 1911–12 year, Cowan moved to Post, Texas, and opened a studio there.[22] She returned to Lubbock for the fall of 1912 and, according to the paper, secured a large music class.[23] Thereafter, she most probably moved again, for her activities were not subsequently documented.

Several new music teachers, all women, settled in Lubbock in or shortly after 1910, and each came to play a significant role in the local music education effort during the second decade of the century. These included Harriet Brown, Margaret Huff, Mrs. Dell King, Adelaide Summers and Mrs. B. P. Hopkins. Later in the decade Elvira Gelin, Eva Browning, and Mamie Neal also set up teaching studios.

Harriet Brown was first on the list of new music educators to come to Lubbock during the second decade. Her arrival in late summer 1910 was accompanied by the following introduction:

> Miss Harriet Brown will open a music studio in Lubbock: voice and piano. She is a graduate of Elmira College, New York, and the Thomas Normal Training School of Detroit. For the past two years she has been head of the voice department of Whitworth College, Mississippi.[24]

Despite only a few weeks' time until school began, her credentials assured her a class, and it must have been a rather large one judging from the number of recitals — three — given by her pupils during the nine-month school year.[25] So successful was she in her first year in Lubbock that she was appointed teacher of music in the school system for the 1911–12 year, "and will have her studio in the High School Building."[26] Again, her students gave three recitals during the year.[27]

Miss Brown was re-appointed for the 1912–13 school year. That year saw the school system increase the number of associated music teachers to four: Misses Brown, Huff, Campbell, and Cowan. Miss Brown taught in the high school building; the others had teaching studios nearby.[28] She evidently did more than teach music that year, for in November her music class put on a play at the Opera House.[29] The 1913–14 year was her last to be associated with the school system. She did remain in Lubbock, however, until 1919, when she married and returned to New York state.[30]

Margaret Huff, another of the new teachers, was one of Lubbock's most enthusiastic and talented teachers and an absolutely first-rate pianist and musician. She initially came to Lubbock for a one-day visit in 1902. She left impressed enough to vow, "If Lubbock ever gets a railroad, I'm coming back."[31] True to her word she returned in 1910 intending to open a studio and now fully qualified to do so; in the intervening years she earned a Bachelor of Music degree with a piano major at the American Conservatory of Music in Chicago, and followed that with six months of post-graduate work in Italy. She also possessed six years experience as a teacher of voice and instrumental music.[32] Initially, she opened her studio not in Lubbock but in Hale Center, where she taught two years. Then, in August 1912, she placed an advertisement in *The Lubbock Avalanche*:

Margaret Huff

Teacher of Piano

Will Open Studio Sept. 2nd.[33]

And her arrival in Lubbock was heralded by the following notice:

> Miss Margaret Huff, who has been teaching piano in Hale Center the past two years, came down to Lubbock Tuesday and will make Lubbock her home in the future. She has an ad in this issue of the *Avalanche*. Look it up. She instructed a class of twenty-two members the past year in Hale Center, and comes to Lubbock highly recommended.[34]

Little did the editor know then that a new era was about to begin in music education in Lubbock, for not only would Margaret Huff become one of the most influential teachers, she would also remain in Lubbock long enough — almost five decades — to leave a lasting legacy. Her ability, recognized quickly during her first year of teaching in Lubbock, led to an appointment by the Lubbock school system as one of the music teachers for the 1913–14 school year; she would retain her connection with the school system for many years. Her work that year culminated in a series of recitals by her students. A guest at one of them wrote an account for the newspaper that appraised the teacher and explained her success:

> Miss Huff may be justly proud of her year's work. Her pupils show wonderful progress made since the beginning of the fall term. Miss Huff uses the art of music as a means of intellectual, aesthetic, and moral culture, and in a characteristic manner succeeds in bringing out the best in every pupil.[35]

On November 14, 1913, she, Mrs. Dell King, and Adelaide Summers put together a musicale for a social entertainment. A review in the newspaper waxed eloquently about Miss Huff's talent, reputation, and artistic sensibilities:

> . . . Miss Margaret Huff accompanied all the above numbers and no comment is needed as to her interpretation and expression except that it was perfect. [Then] she gave the audience a descriptive and analytical illustration of the manner in which that very popular classic by Dvorak, entitled "Humoresque," had been rendered by several professional artists, who lately visited Lubbock, and then gave her own idea of how this masterpiece should be played. The difference was beautifully accented and perceptible even to the lay mind. She generously conceded that the visiting artists were, in their way, correct, but exemplified the point that the rendition of this very popular classic, to be effective, did not entirely depend upon the perfect reproduction of the rhythm and harmony, [but] required a cultivated and refined taste to properly produce the hidden sentiment the composer intended to convey. Her remarks and illustrations were instructive to the music lover as well as entertaining to all, and left nothing to doubt that she deserves the well-earned recognition as holding a place in musical culture, its ethics and performance.[36]

Miss Huff's artistic credo was outlined in that review, namely, that a cultivated and refined taste is the highest musical aspiration and is necessary to produce the hidden sentiment of a composition.

During her early years in Lubbock she frequently took the stage as a solo performer. One particularly colorful appraisal was uttered by George Slaughter, a pioneer rancher in West Texas: "Say, girl, what are you doing here? I've heard [the great Polish pianist] Paderewski, and he ain't got nothing on you."[37]

In 1914 Miss Huff directed a group of twenty to twenty-five singers in a performance of Alfred Gaul's sacred cantata "The Holy City," given in the Opera House. This may have occurred in association with her musical duties at Lubbock's First Presbyterian Church, where, beginning upon her arrival in Lubbock in 1912, she was pianist and later organist. (The church obtained an organ in 1932.)

Miss Huff went to Egypt in 1919 for a two-year stint teaching music in Cairo at a Presbyterian college, the American Mission College for Girls.[38] She returned to the U.S. in the fall of 1921 and to Lubbock in July 1922.[39] Except for a brief sojourn to North Carolina, she spent the next thirty-nine years sharing her art and her knowledge with the young people of Lubbock, teaching voice, piano, and organ. Those who knew her well described her as "a very, very good teacher, well-trained and sincere," "a fine musician," "a disciplinarian," and "very loving."[40]

In June 1913, the newspaper reported that "Mrs. Dell King, of Loraine, Texas, was here . . . looking for a location."[41] She apparently found what she was looking for; within a month she had settled in Lubbock and introduced herself to the community with the following notice:

> Mrs. Dell King wishes to announce to the public that she will teach near the school this coming term.
>
> Mrs. King teaches piano, harmony, theory and musical history and will also organize choral classes of different ages.
>
> Terms $4 per month. 40 minutes [per lesson] and two lessons per week. All music pupils are required to be a member of musical clubs and choral class without extra charge . . .[42]

The reader's eyebrow is permitted to rise slightly at the prospect of two private piano lessons, plus class (club) instruction in harmony, theory and music history, plus choral singing — all for less than a dollar per week! However, that was the going rate. Little else is known about Mrs. King save that she remained in Lubbock at least four years, becoming one of the music teachers attached to the school system in 1916–17.[43]

Mrs. Adelaide Summers began her Lubbock teaching career in the fall of 1913, at that time placing an advertisement in the newspaper offering instruction in "voice culture and the art of singing."[44] While her background and credentials are unknown, the community's need for a first-rate singer and singing teacher to replace Philip Baer made her acceptance assured and swift. Hence, even though she did not advertise her services until October, she met no difficulty assembling a music class. The following spring her students were presented in recital, and the piano accompaniments were provided by colleagues Margaret Huff and Mrs. King — an act of devotion, acceptance and cooperation.[45] Not much else is known about Mrs. Summers, except that in 1918 she extended her talent to conducting the orchestra of the Methodist Sunday School.[46]

Mrs. B. P. Hopkins, teacher of piano and voice, was living in Lubbock as early as 1914, but may not have opened a teaching studio until 1919, when she was one of four piano teachers appointed to the school system.[47] She and her pupils gave numerous recitals at least through the 1922–23 year.

Mrs. Elvira Gelin became active in teaching music in Lubbock around 1918. She was a music teacher in the school system during the 1918–19 year, and by the following year had become Principal of the Music Department.[48] She taught piano and voice.

Several of these private teachers remained active in Lubbock for many years. In fact, the vigor and amount of music education and the number of active music teachers after World War I demands further attention. The dramatic increase in population in the 1920's, from about 4,000 to over 20,000, and the attendant increase in music education programs and musical associations of various kinds, will constitute a rather full study by themselves.[49]

RECITAL PROGRAMS

Recital programs of the period further illustrate the state of music education in early Lubbock. Given below are two, representing Nancy Patterson's class in 1908 (Figure 14), and Elvira Gelin's in 1919 (Figure 15).[50] They reveal a cross-section of the kind of repertory available to music teachers during the first twenty years of this century and, as well, the musical tastes and inclinations of the teachers. For example, Nancy Patterson leaned toward "classical" fare, with music by Richard Wagner (Nos. 7 and 10), Gioacchino Rossini (18), and George Bizet (15), while other teachers including Mrs. Gelin often chose lighter fare. However, that should not be interpreted as criticism of musical taste, for the classical masters wrote little for children and even less specifically for beginners. The lighter pieces varied from sweet and sentimental to lively and descriptive, and were immediately appealing to youngsters. If most of that repertoire seems unfamiliar today, it is what publishers were making available to music teachers during the first two decades of the century.

The Patterson program did not list performers for any of its nineteen numbers, but was well varied, as all these recitals were, including pieces for an orchestra (whether composed of students isn't clear) and a chorus, vocal and instrumental solos and duets, as well as readings (Nos. 6 and 11). Mrs. Gelin's Commencement Recital of 1919 was divided into two parts: the primary and grammar school students first, the high schoolers after intermission. The program, dressed up by assistance from Mr. and Mrs. Gelin and a Mrs. Von Rosenberg, consisted of twenty-five numbers, typical of these programs.

The students were pianists, violinists, or singers; at this time those were the only areas where private instruction was available. Class recitals displayed the talents of twenty to thirty pupils, each performing usually only one or two numbers. The repertoire consisted in large measure of the musical literature then available for and attractive to youngsters.

Like modern audiences for student recitals, these no doubt included many proud parents. But in a young town eager for arts of all kinds, appreciative music lovers probably attended as well, deriving reward from the performers' efforts, especially from the adults and the more advanced students. Thus, these recitals contributed to the cultural welfare of the community.

One other note regarding the music teachers: a spirit of cooperation rather than rivalry seems to have characterized their interaction. "Pulling together for the common good" might well have been their motto, so willing were they, as a group, to assist one another or the city when a high-grade musical effort was needed. One memorable and successful such cooperative effort was in connection with a trades display show put on by Lubbock's merchants in October 1913. Miss Campbell coordinated a musical program, and her colleagues responded enthusiastically. The newspaper reviewed the musical portion of the event:

> The Trades Display given at the Lyric last Tuesday night under the direction of Miss Lula Campbell was quite a success . . . The instrumental music furnished by Miss Huff and Mrs. King and the vocal solos by Mrs. Summers and the vocal duet by Mrs. King and Mrs. Summers were very beautiful and greatly appreciated . . .[51]

At another event, in May 1914, the program of the seven clubs making up the Lubbock County Federation of Clubs included, in addition to welcoming speeches, reports, and a business meeting, music by Harriet Brown, Margaret Huff, Mrs. B. P. Hopkins, and a Mrs. Duering.[52] The teachers often assisted their colleagues, as when in May 1913 pupils of Adelaide Summers, the town's leading voice teacher, were accompanied

Programme

Friday Night Feb. 7, at Band Hall.

By Miss Patterson and her music class, assisted by Orchestra.

1 "Waltz" (overture)   Orchestra.

2 "Dear Old College Days," Chorus from Burgomaster.

3 "Faust,"   Piano Duett.

4 "Intermezzo,"   Engleman.

5 "Valse,"   Humoresque.

6 "Selection from Yankee Tourist.

7 "Under The Double Eagle,"   Wagner.

8 "Golden Leaf Polka,"   Trombone and Piano.

9 "The Land of Swallows,"   Masini.

10 "March,"   Tanihausur.

11 "Reading." (The Bear Story).

12 "The Rural Wedding,"   Piano Duett.

13 "Gallop Militare,"   Bohm,

14 "Dreaming,"   Orchestra.

15 "Habarnara."   Selection from Carmen.

16 "Vocal,"   Scherzo.

17 "Polka De Concert."

18 "Tancred Overture,"   Rossina.

19 "Orchestra."

Figure 14. Recital Program.

— *The Avalanche*, February 7, 1908, p. 1

Commencement Recital

Given by the Pupils of

Mrs. Elvira M. Wennerskold Gelin

--PART I--

Grammar School

Little Boy Blue .... Engleman
Edith Peek and Rebecca Quinn.
Curly Locks .... L. E. orcte
Beulah Moore (Primary Dept.)
Holiday Two Step .... Read
Edith Thomas.
Rain Pitter-Patters .... Theo. Dutton
Doyle Blankenship
Dancing Flowers .... Edward Holst
Cecil, Flora and Edna Sims.
Fairy Polka .... Spindler
Bobbie Wilkinson
Les Marguerites .... La Fontain
Flora Sims
The Whispering Leaves .... Chas. Tanley
Mmes. Von Rosenberg, Ellis, Rylander and Gelin.
Pixies Good Night Song .... A. L. Brown
Mellie Thomas
Rondoletto (C major and C Minor) ....Burgmuller
Edna Sims
The Dance of the Brownies ....E. F. Hamman
Rebecca Quinn
Edelweiss Glide Waltz .... E. F. Vanderbeck
Loyce Mills.
Summer .... Lichner
Annette Hussey
(Ten Minutes Intermission)

--PART II--

High School

The Dance of the June Bugs .... Holst
Edith and Ruby Peek
The Harp at Midnight (Nocturne) .... V. B. Aubert
Lillian Cunningham.
When the Heart is Young .... Dudley Buck
Ethel Summers
Polka Brillante .... F. Spindler
Waldene Chauncey
Sonata No. 2 G Major (Mentoso; Poco Andante
Allegro Moderato) .... Bohm
Ruth Hussey and Mrs. Gelin
Chanson Des Alps (Fantasia De Concert) ....Ryder
Cecil Sims
Good-Bye .... Tosti
Mrs. Von Rosenberg
Pearl and Diamonds .... Lange
Ida Lou Ellis
(a) Third Mazurka .... Ben. Godard
(b) "Home Longing" .... Jungman
Ruth Hussey.
Babylon .... M. Watson
Mr. Gelin
Les Sylphes .... Bachman
Ida Lou Ellis and Mrs. Gelin

Figure 15. Recital Program.
— *The Lubbock Avalanche,* May 8, 1919, p. 24

in recital not by other students but by two of the town's leading pianists, Margaret Huff and Mrs. Dell King.[53] And, of course, all proceeds from recitals by these performers and their music classes were always put to worthy purposes: the city churches' charitable causes, school buildings and equipment, and other community needs.

In sum, the music teachers were frequently called upon to help the city, and they always responded generously. They provided entertainment, produced benefit recitals for worthy causes, and of course improved the quality of Lubbock's cultural life. It was Lubbock's blessing to have in its music teachers such concerned and civic-minded citizens.

LOCAL THEATER

Another source of cultural entertainment was provided by the town's actors and actresses. Even in Lubbock's earliest days, theatrical events were a favorite entertainment, but it was not until the time of the Lubbock 1906 Band that an organized effort to present dramas to the community on a regular basis occurred. As noted in Chapter 4, that band often included a light play or a farce on its programs. Between August 1907 and February 1908 (after which time the band seems to have ceased), four plays were given: "Jumbo Jum," "Cato, Leb and Col. Spruceup," "The Honor of a Cowboy," and "Tony the Convict." Townspeople participated in these productions, and, perhaps inspired by their success, formed an independent organization, the Hawthorne Dramatic Club, in January 1908. According to the newspaper, "The Club expects to put on plays and give the proceeds to public enterprises."[54] In April, the Club mounted its premier production: "Because I Love You." The cast of eleven executed the performance "in a manner that would be highly complimentary to professional stage players"; the play earned almost $100, all set aside for the establishment of a fire department.[55]

It appears that the Hawthorne Dramatic Club did not perform again, and only sporadic local efforts at plays are documented for the years immediately following: none in 1909, two in 1910, and one in 1911, including such favorites as "Her Father's Crime" and "Mrs. Wiggs of the Cabbage Patch." The re-organized Lubbock Band, assisted by non-band members from the community, added two plays in 1912, "Uncle Josh" and "The Face at the Window." Lubbock High School students put on one in 1912 and another in 1913. And to benefit the Baptist Ladies Aid Society, local talent came together once again in 1914 to present "Dot, the Miner's Daughter."[56] Compared to the musical efforts, the number of theatrical productions dropped considerably after 1908. The explanation is probably that, after the coming of the railroad, in the fall of 1909, the Opera House continuously presented traveling dramatic companies and so satisfied the community's need for such entertainment. However, local actors and actresses eagerly took to the stage whenever a charitable cause could benefit from their services. Lubbock's thespians, like the musicians, were always ready to contribute their talents for the benefit of their city. Meanwhile, it would be many years before community theater would thrive in Lubbock, after the era of the circuit players had passed.

LOCAL ORCHESTRAS

Three Lubbock orchestras captured the spotlight during the earliest years of the 1900's. All were small ensembles of fewer than ten players, made up of strings, brass, and piano. Apparently the first since the 1890's was formed by Nancy Patterson in 1908. Its debut took place on a recital by her music class on February 7.[57] While the newspaper didn't reveal the composition of the orchestra at its debut, it listed the membership for a concert on July 24, 1908:

> Mr. Bristol, violin
> Nancy Patterson, violin
> S. C. Wilson, trombone
> E. A. Carlock, cornet
> Hattie McGee, piano[58]

Little else is known about this orchestra, save that it did not continue beyond the summer of 1908, most likely disbanding because E. A. Carlock moved to Paducah, Texas, in late July and Hattie McGee went off to college in the fall.[59]

As if to fill the void, Lula Campbell's orchestra commenced music making in August 1908, at which time, according to the newspaper, it was composed of (only surnames given): Campbell, Graham, Wheelock, and Neal.[60] This organization gave at least seven performances between August 1908 and July 1910, mostly for parties or charitable events. After July 1910, no more was heard from it. A new orchestra, formed early in 1910 and known as the Lubbock Concert Orchestra, seems to have displaced it. This orchestra included:

Fred Hettler, violin and director
H. B. Thomas, 1st violin
J. E. Kane, 1st cornet
Edgar Inmon, 2nd cornet
S. C. Wilson, trombone
Willie Cowan, piano[61]

Its debut, at a town meeting at the Orpheum Opera House on February 19, 1910, was evidently quite a success. The newspaper enthused: "This orchestra has practiced but little [Dr. Kane, a veterinarian, having moved to Lubbock only a few weeks earlier] and it was surprising to hear them render difficult pieces with apparent ease; and their renditions were met with rounds of applause."[62]

The Lubbock Concert Orchestra, also known simply as the Lubbock Orchestra, performed numerous times in the ensuing months — for Sunday School meetings, lodge meetings, Sunday School classes, even the Lubbock High School Commencement — until serious illness in the fall forced Dr. Kane to withdraw.[63] The orchestra regrouped in the summer of 1911 and is known to have played for church socials and dances. In the summer of 1912 the orchestra entered into an agreement with E. M. McElroy, manager of both the Opera House and a new venture that summer, the Airdome, an open-air movie theater (Chapter 3). Apparently McElroy invited the orchestra to become the specialty entertainment on Friday evenings, advertising that "the Lovers of Good Music will be highly entertained by the Lubbock Orchestra at the LYRIC [Airdome], Friday night. Very Interesting Program."[64] During the fall and winter, the orchestra occasionally worked as the specialty act for traveling companies and also played for dances, its reputation even earning out-of-town engagements.[65]

A typical, handsome advertisement for the Airdome (Figure 16) tells of the orchestra's link to the movie theater again during the summer of 1913.[66] At ten cents' admission, however, the orchestra, if paid at all, would accumulate wealth only very slowly. For financial or other reasons, this orchestra seems to have put away its instruments with the end of summer 1913. While issues of the newspaper are available for another year, no further mention of the Lubbock Orchestra is made. Unavailability of papers from July 1914 to August 1918 casts a veil over all orchestral activity throughout that entire four-year period.

Of the repertoire these orchestras played, unfortunately, only one program is available, that for the debut of Nancy Patterson's orchestra in February 1908 (See Figure 14). The group played an overture, a piece

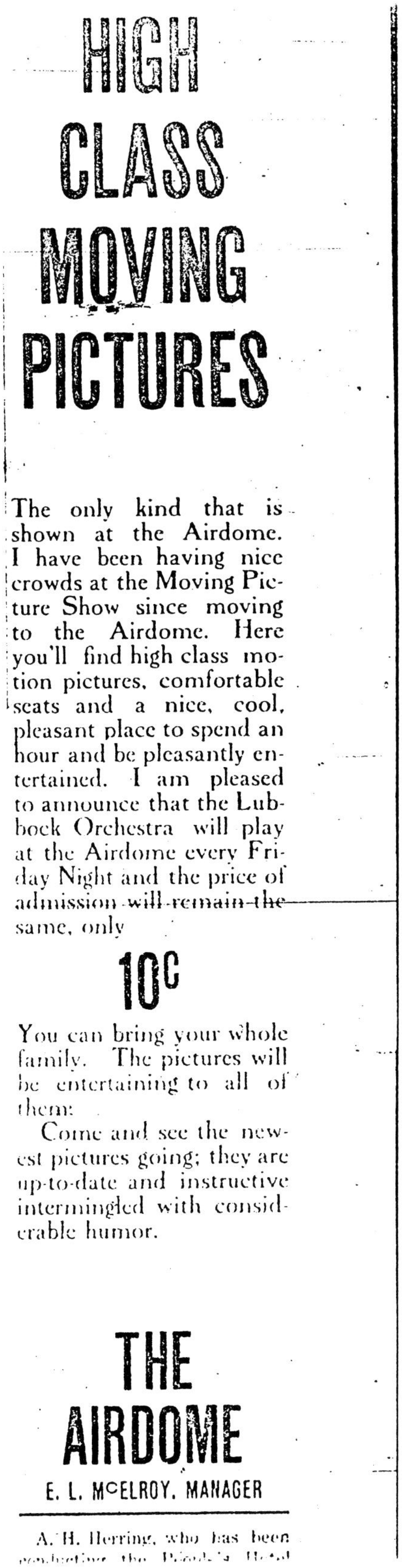

HIGH CLASS MOVING PICTURES

The only kind that is shown at the Airdome. I have been having nice crowds at the Moving Picture Show since moving to the Airdome. Here you'll find high class motion pictures, comfortable seats and a nice, cool, pleasant place to spend an hour and be pleasantly entertained. I am pleased to announce that the Lubbock Orchestra will play at the Airdome every Friday Night and the price of admission will remain the same, only

10¢

You can bring your whole family. The pictures will be entertaining to all of them.

Come and see the newest pictures going; they are up-to-date and instructive intermingled with considerable humor.

THE AIRDOME

E. L. McELROY, MANAGER

A. H. Herring, who has been conducting the Pickwick Hotel

Figure 16. Advertisement for the Airdome.
— *The Lubbock Avalanche,* June 19, 1913, p. 8

called "Dreaming," a Polka, and an arrangement of the overture to Rossini's opera *Tancredi*.[67] It is likely that other orchestra programs included classical music also, but most probably consisted of arrangements of popular songs and dances, since these orchestras served mainly at parties and dances. An effort to establish a genuine symphony orchestra would not occur until 1928 and would not succeed until 1946.

PUBLIC SCHOOL MUSIC

Although the Lubbock High School assembled its first band in 1916 and its first orchestra in 1917 or 1918, music did not become a formal part of the curriculum until the 1920's. During that decade, coursework in music theory and music appreciation was introduced along with other ensembles, all for credit. However, private teaching of music had gained entry into the Lubbock public schools several years earlier.

In 1910, the Lubbock School Board began to play a role in the promotion of musical study and performance. It must have been seen as a progressive sign when the Board announced that for the 1910–11 year:

> . . . two music teachers shall teach in the building, so that the pupils who wish to take music lessons will not be compelled to leave the grounds or the building for this purpose. It is thought that this will be much better, and will be generally approved of by the patrons of the school. The board chose as the music teachers in the school building Misses Cowan and Campbell.[68]

The lessons were private, paid by the students directly to the teachers who, apparently, were not otherwise paid by the School Board or considered part of the faculty. Lessons were given on the school grounds for the safety and convenience of the children and also to underscore the school system's commitment to providing instruction in music.

Four teachers were available for private lessons during the 1912–13 year, but because the building could accommodate only one (Harriet Brown), the other three (Margaret Huff, Lula Campbell, and Willie Cowan) taught in studios nearby.[69]

The Music Department of the school system continued to expand to meet an ever-increasing demand. By the 1919–20 school year music was taught in three buildings and by five teachers.[70] The school for grades first-to-second contained two music rooms with a piano in each. The George M. Hunt school for grades third-to-seventh also had two music rooms with a piano in each. The Lubbock High School housed the main facilities for instruction in music. A notice in the newspaper informed parents what they could expect from the 1919–20 school session:

> The Conservatory of Music of the Lubbock High School announces the session of 1919–20 commencing Sept. 8th.
>
> The faculty will include four piano teachers, one violin and one expression teacher. Tuition will be [for] 8 lessons, $6.00 per month, two lessons a week; two from one family, $11.00.
>
> Piano teachers are Miss Eva Browning, Mrs. [B. P.] Hopkins and Mrs. [Elvira] Gelin . . .
>
> M. M. DUPRE [Superintendent],
>
> Elvira M. Gelin [Principal of the Music Department].[71]

The fourth piano teacher, perhaps as yet unhired, replaced Margaret Huff, who began teaching abroad at this time. The going rate for music lessons was now $6.00 per month for eight (or possibly nine) private lessons plus a class in theory instruction once a week, a widely practiced pedagogical approach.

So large was the number of students taking music lessons during the 1919–20 school year that it took five separate recitals during the month of May to hear them all:

Saturday, May 15, 3:00	Primary pupils
Monday, May 17, 7:30	Advanced pupils
Tuesday, May 18, 7:30	Advanced pupils
Wednesday, May 19, 7:30	Commencement Concert
Friday, May 21, 3:00	Intermediate pupils[72]

It wouldn't be long before such demand led to the introduction of ensembles and formal coursework in music. Music ensembles came next. A band, under the direction of Mr. C. A. Wallace, was organized in 1916, and an orchestra in 1917 or 1918.[73] Music appreciation was introduced into the curriculum in 1925, and the first faculty to offer general music classes were hired shortly thereafter.[74] However, before World War I and even after it, the private music teacher remained the backbone of the school system's music education program.

It was customary for *The Lubbock Avalanche* to list each year the teachers of the Lubbock school system. Below is a list of music teachers for those years between 1910 and 1920 where issues of the newspaper were available:

1910–11	Willie Cowan and Lula Campbell
1911–12	Harriet Brown and Lula Campbell
1912–13	Harriet Brown, Margaret Huff, Lula Campbell and Willie Cowan
1913–14	Margaret Huff and Harriet Brown [perhaps others also]
1916–17	Margaret Huff, Vera Murfee, Miss Carter and Mrs. Dell King
1917–18[75]	Margaret Huff, Vera Murfee, and Eva Browning
1918–19	Eva Browning and Elvira Gelin [perhaps others also]
1919–20	Eva Browning, Mrs. B. P. Hopkins, Mrs. Cole and Elvia Gelin, Principal of the Music Department

CHAPTER 7

Lubbock's Cultural Heritage

In less than three decades, from 1891 through World War I, Lubbock grew from an outpost on the high plains of West Texas, inhabited by a handful of hardy pioneers, to a booming small city of nearly 4,000 inhabitants. Along with growth in public and private institutions and the economy came the social and cultural developments which have been the focus of this study.

Culture and the arts flourished in Lubbock, provided by its own citizens with artistic talents, its music teachers, and the great annual influx of traveling entertainers. During the first three decades, Lubbock numbered among its residents many with artistic abilities, predominantly in music. Especially noteworthy were bandsmen Smylie Wilson, N. C. Bishop, and Monte Bowron, and music teachers Nancy Patterson, Lula Campbell, Philip Baer, Harriet Brown, Margaret Huff, Mrs. Dell King, Adelaide Summers, Mrs. B. P. Hopkins, Elvira Gelin, Eva Browning, and Mamie Neal.

The most profound effect on the cultural life of the city came with the railroad, which enhanced both the quantity and quality of Lubbock's arts. After the advent of the railroad to Lubbock in fall 1909, the city became a stop on the circuits crisscrossing the country carrying culture to rural America. In 1905, only three traveling groups made their way to Lubbock; in the nine months from September 1913 to May 1914, eighteen did. While the iron horse made possible Lubbock's exposure to outside performers and productions, E. M. McElroy, manager of the town's Opera House, made the events happen. Under his direction the Opera House hosted dramatic presentations by professional companies and local thespians. It hosted concerts and recitals by both touring professionals and local musicians, and showed moving pictures every available evening. Citizens gathered at the Opera House for meetings of fraternal and other clubs, town councils, political rallies, lectures on everything from religion to osteopathy, dances, carnivals, vaudeville shows, and church services. McElroy and his Opera House made a contribution to the community that can scarcely be overstated.

From the town's earliest years, and perhaps in response to their city's geographical isolation, Lubbock's parents wanted their children well-educated in the fine arts, especially music. Happily, the school system complied, promoting the study of music, albeit, during the early years, via lessons by private teachers rather than general music classes available to all students. Nevertheless, two music teachers gave private lessons in the schools in 1910, a figure that increased to five by 1919. Early Lubbock had no difficulty attracting distinguished music educators. In the days immediately after the founding of the town, those pioneers trained in music saw to the musical needs of the community and the instruction of the children. After 1905, with Nancy Patterson and Lula Campbell, the music education effort was in the hands of professionals. Most of the teachers possessed college degrees in music, and several, such as Margaret Huff and Harriet Brown, embarked upon post-baccalaureate study to further their musical and pedagogical skills. These private teachers of piano, violin, and voice exposed their pupils to instruction in choral singing, theory, music history, and musicianship, thereby establishing in Lubbock a substantial pedagogical program and an approach to music education widely practiced at the time.

Other cultural resources included the churches with their heavy reliance upon music, various orchestras that encouraged edification of the mind as well as movement of the feet, singing groups, theatrical efforts by local actors and actresses whenever taking the stage would benefit a worthy cause, and, last but by no means least, Lubbock's bands.

Lubbock's five early bands figured prominently on the cultural scene. The small pioneer community of under 1,000 inhabitants before the railroad came could scarcely find the financial wherewithal to support a band; three came and went in rapid succession. A Lubbock of 3,500 in 1912, however, proved that it was up to the challenge. Once the city was able to attract and retain the services of as competent and professional a band director/teacher as Monte Bowron, in 1913, the Lubbock Cowboy Band would become, through regular weekly summer concerts in the bandstand, the most visible feature on Lubbock's musical horizon. Its regional reputation went unchallenged, and admiration for the organization extended well beyond West Texas. The band favored Lubbock with America's most beloved music until World War I brought about its demise.

In the midst of it all, throwing the full weight of his newspaper behind Lubbock's cultural welfare, was Editor James Dow. Interested in the cultural growth of his community as well as its physical growth, he appears as a star performer throughout the pages of this history.

All these elements — the music teachers, public schools, churches, bands, orchestras, Band Hall and Opera House with diverse and numerous attractions, and newspaper — contributed significantly to the health and welfare of culture, the arts, and entertainment in Lubbock. Each helped lay a solid foundation upon which to build a great cultural edifice in the years after World War I. Owing to that foundation, the influence of Texas Tech University after 1925, and an enormous increase in population, Lubbock has today become one of the great cultural centers in West Texas.

Nevertheless, it is remarkable that culture developed as it did in Lubbock prior to World War I. After all, in the 1890's Lubbock was a mere isolated dot on the plains of West Texas, a flat, barren, windswept spot with few natural resources or attractions. The main occupation of the day was survival, and we might be forgiven for expecting the pioneers, in difficult times, to lose sight of culture and the arts. Yet the record is clear; they didn't. Because of the high value that Lubbock's early citizens placed upon building culture, Lubbock's struggle for a cultural identity was a genuine success story.

Cultural activity is a measure of a town's health, a mirror of its social conscience. This cultural view, perhaps, has added another dimension to previous studies of early Lubbock, exposing Lubbock for what it was and still is: a community vitally concerned with the finer things of life, with culture and the arts.

Appendix A

KNOWN CULTURAL/ENTERTAINMENT/OTHER EVENTS
AT THE BAND HALL, 1907–1909

(Titles of dramas given where known):

ENTRY #	DATE	EVENT
1907		
1.	8/1	Mollie Bailey Circus
2.	8/5	Moving pictures
3.	8/10	Concert: Lubbock 1906 Band
4.	8/13	Concert: Effie Kelley
5.	8/16	Moving pictures
6.	9/27	Recital: Philip Baer and music class
7.	10/12	Recital: Nancy Patterson's music class
8.	10/19	Concert: Lubbock 1906 Band
9.	11/14	Concert: Lubbock 1906 Band
10.	11/23	Recital: Nancy Patterson's music class
11.	11/28	Concert: Benefit of Cemetery Association
12.	12/20	Drama: Benefit of Baptist Church "A Ruined Life" (local talent)
13.	12/late	Drama: Lubbock 1906 Band "The Honor of a Cow Boy"
1908		
14.	2/7	Recital: Nancy Patterson's music class
15.	2/17	Concert: Lubbock 1906 Band
16.	2/22	Drama: Lubbock 1906 Band "Tony the Convict"
17.	4/7	Drama: Hawthorne Dramatic Club "Because I Love You" (local talent)
18.	5/1	Recital: Lula Campbell's music class
19.	7/24	Recital: Nancy Patterson's orchestra et al
20.	8/28–8/29	Recital: Philip Baer's music class
21.	9/7	Lecture (religious): Rev. M. M. Smith
22.	9/11	Rhyme Social: Woman's Home Mission Society
23.	10/4	Lecture (religious): Rev. M. M. Smith
24.	12/10	Recital: Mrs. George Beatty (elocution)
1909		
25.	1/2	Recital: Lula Campbell's orchestra and class
26.	1/12	Meeting: Odd Fellows
27.	1/31	Lecture (religious): Rev. E. Robinson

28.	2/24–2/25	Dramas: Traveling Company (unnamed)
		2/24: "Zeke, the Country Boy"
		2/25: "The Deserter"
29.	5/12	Meeting: The town's carpenters
30.	11/25	Banquet: Odd Fellows
31.	12/17	Meeting: Lubbock Concert Band

Appendix B

KNOWN CULTURAL/ENTERTAINMENT/OTHER EVENTS AT THE ORPHEUM

OPERA HOUSE (Titles of dramas given where known):

ENTRY #	DATE	EVENT
1909		
1.	Week of 4/12	Dramas: Angell's Comedians* "The Devil" "Paid in Full" "Way Down East" "The Counterfeiters"
2.	4/21	Meeting: Commercial Club Secretaries and Newspaper Men
3.	5/14	Fundraiser: Woman's Home Mission Society
4.	5/21	Concert: Benefit of Presbyterian Church, Plainview
5.	5/28	Dance: Benefit of Lubbock Baseball Team
6.	6/2	Banquet: Woodmen of the World
7.	6/6–6/7	Lubbock High School Commencement Exercises
8.	6/24	Meeting: Masons of Yellow House Lodge
9.	7/8	Lecture (religious): Bishop Garrett of Dallas
10.	7/20	Fundraiser: Ladies of the First Presbyterian Church
11.	8/12—	Moving Pictures: Every available night
12.	8/15	Lecture (religious): Rev. John Foster of New Orleans
13.	8/24	Concert: Mary Bell
14.	9/12	Lecture (religious): Bro. Carmey's temperance lecture
15.	9/15–9/18	Carnival: (Company unknown)
16.	Week of 11/8	Dramas: Angell's Comedians 11/10: "The Duke's Daughter"
17.	11/23	Lecture (religious): Homer T. Wilson
18.	Week of 11/29	Dramas: Howard Stock Company 11/30: "Samson of Yale" 12/1: "In the Shadow of the Gallows" 12/2: "Lena Rivers"
19.	12/11	Concert: Benefit of First Presbyterian Church
20.	12/15–12/17	Dramas: Woodward Stock Company 12/15: "Brought to Justice" 12/16: "The Boss of the House" 12/17: "Sunset Land"
1910		
21.	1/10–1/11	Drama: Benefit of Lubbock Fire Department "Her Father's Crime" (local talent)
22.	Week of 1/17	Vaudeville: Ford & Miller Company

* It is uncertain whether Angell's Comedians performed at the Band Hall or at the Opera House (if completed by April 12).

23.	Week of 1/24	Vaudeville: Sampson & Walworth Company
24.	Week of 1/31	Dramas: Alhambra Stock Company
25.	2/11	Drama: (Company unnamed)
		"The Missouri Girl"
26.	2/16	Rally: Citizens rally regarding state of the city
27.	3/4–3/5	Vaudeville: Grace Huntington Vaudeville Company
28.	3/20	Church Services: Episcopal Church
29.	March/April	Baraca Class of Methodist Church, 9:45 A.M. every Sunday
30.	4/16	Meeting: Mass meeting of Lubbock citizens
31.	4/19–4/20	Lectures (religious): Dr. George Gildert Bancroft
32.	4/21	Concert: Lubbock High School Commencement Exercises
33.	4/29	Concert: Girls Glee Club of Hereford College
34.	Week of 5/2	Dramas: The Woods Sisters and Company
		5/2: "A Daughter of Dixie"
		5/3: "The Parisian Princess"
		5/4: "A Gay Deceiver"
		5/5: "Her Fatal Marriage"
		5/6: "Worm Wood"
		5/7 matinee: "For Mother's Sake"
		5/7: "Thelma"
35.	Week of 5/9	Dramas: Sanford Dodge Company
36.	5/9	Actor: Frederick Wilson
37.	5/10–5/12	Lectures (religious): John R. Charlesworth
38.	5/12 (?)	Political rally: William Poindexter, candidate for governor
39.	5/28	Program by Bert Carter of Hereford College
40.	5/30 and 6/10	Drama: Benefit of Odd Fellows and Rebekahs
		"The Breakers" (local talent)
41.	6/10	Meeting: Lubbock Commercial Club
42.	6/16	Recital: Nancy Patterson's music class
43.	6/24	Recital: Lula Campbell's music class
44.	7/?	Dramas: Cutler's Theatre (in Opera House ?)
45.	7/28–7/29	Carnival: A grand merchants' carnival
46.	9/6	Recital: Philip Baer's music class
47.	9/16	Lecture: Dr. Pennock on osteopathy
48.	Week of 10/10*	Drama: Albert Taylor Company
49.	10/20	Concert: Eureka Glee Club (Lyceum Course)
50.	10/21	Lecture (religious): Rev. Edwin Weary
51.	11/6	Meeting: A temperance mass meeting
52.	11/21	Vaudeville: Earl and Mayme Cox (Lyceum Course)
53.	11/23–11/24	Dramas: Maudena's Musical Comedy

1911

54.	2/3	Drama: Benefit of the Lubbock Library
		"Mrs. Wiggs of the Cabbage Patch" (local talent)
55.	2/9	Concert: (Performing group unknown, Lyceum Course)
56.	2/18	Lecture: "Play Ball" by Clark
57.	2/25	Meeting: Lubbock County Prohibition Club
58.	3/16	Concert: Columbian Quartette (Lyceum Course)
59.	Week of 3/27	Dramas: Albert Taylor Company
60.	5/7	Rally: Lubbock County Prohibition Club

---

* Dode-Fisk Show on 10/3 was probably under canvas and not in the Opera House.

61.	5/16	Concert: Schubert Club (in Opera House?)
62.	7/17	Concert: Austin College (Vocal) Quartette
63.	Week of 10/9 *	Dramas: Albert Taylor Company

1912

64.	1/26	Moving Pictures: Benefit of the Lubbock Library
65.	1/29–1/31	Dramas: Russell's Merrymakers "The Shepherd of the Hills"
66.	2/21	Drama: Bert Leigh and Company "The Man on the Box"
67.	3/14–3/15	Moving Pictures: Moran-Attell boxing match
68.	3/27–3/28	Dramas: Lasserre Comedy Company "Two Men and a Girl"
	4/1–4/2**	"When We Were Twenty-One"
69.	9/10***	Drama: Albert Taylor Company "The Game"
70.	10/11	Drama: The Lubbock Band "Uncle Josh"
71.	10/15	Fundraiser: Missionary Society of the Methodist Church
72.	10/19	Drama: Oscar Graham Company "The Stumbling Block"
73.	11/5	Drama: Gilmore Brown and Company "The House of a Thousand Candles"
74.	11/15	Drama: The Lubbock Band "The Face at the Window"
75.	11/18–11/20	Dramas: Angell's Comedians 11/18: "Anita"
76.	11/26	Drama: Jones & Crane "The Servant in the House"
77.	11/29	Drama: Lubbock High School presentation
78.	12/6	Concert: Ellen Beach Yaw, singer
79.	12/12	Drama: Gaskill & MacVitty "The Rosary"
80.	12/20	Concert: Alliene Marie Brazelton, singer

1913

81.	1/2	Drama: Hilliard Wright and Company "Hamlet"
82.	1/15–1/16	Dramas: The Whittaker Company
83.	2/12****	Drama: C. S. Primrose "Paid in Full"
84.	5/5	Moving pictures; dance

---

* The Mollie Bailey Circus in June, the Campbell Brothers Tent Show on 9/14, and the "101 Ranch Real Wild West" show on 10/25 were all under canvas.

** In May, McElroy had erected on the north side of the square an open-air theatre for moving pictures, which during the summer would be more pleasant than a closed building. All moving pictures during the summers of 1912 and 1913 were shown there, and are therefore not included in the above listing. Nightly moving pictures resumed at the Opera House in the fall.

*** Cole Brothers Shows on 9/26, Kit Carson's "Buffalo Ranch Wild West and Trained Wild Animal Exhibition" on 10/12, the Eiler Show's "Rip Van Winkle" on 10/14, and the Blondin Show's "The Cowboy, Indian and the Lady" on 10/28 were all under canvas.

**** Issues of *The Lubbock Avalanche* from 1/9/1913 through 5/1/1913 are unavailable; hence, no other information on activities at the Opera House is known.

85.	5/12	Drama:
		"Those Dreadful Times" (Hale Center talent)
86.	5/21	Concert: The Strollers (Male quartet)
87.	6/2	First Monday Trades Day: Dinner
88.	6/16	Recital: Ruth Wingo, pianist
		Mina Farris, reader
89.	6/13—	The regular 2nd Friday night (of the month) dance
90.	7/7	Fundraiser: Cumberland Ladies Aid Society
91.	8/4	Dance: First Monday Trades Day event
92.	9/3–9/4	Dramas: Oscar Graham and Company
		9/3: "A Prince of His Race"
		9/4: "The Higher Law"
93.	10/7	Concert: The Chicago Ladies Orchestra (Lyceum Course)
94.	10/14	Concert: Trades Display event (local talent)
95.	10/20–10/26	Drama: Dougherty Stock Company
96.	10/27	Concert: The Play Singers (Lyceum Course)*
97.	11/5	Drama: Dubinsky Bros., Inc.
		"The Price She Paid"
98.	11/10–11/15	Dramas: Angell's Comedians
		11/14: "Ishmael"
		11/15 matinee: "A Southern Romance"
		11/15: "Easy Jim"
99.	11/26	Drama: The Lubbock High School
		"The Varsity Coach"
100.	12/5	Drama:
		"Sis Perkins"
101.	12/8	Concert (?): The University Girls (Lyceum Course)
102.	12/10–12/11	Dramas: Albert Taylor Company
103.	12/29	Drama:
		"Sunbonnet Sue"

1914

104.	1/8	Concert: Le Barge Music Company (Lyceum Course)
105.	1/17	Drama:
		"The Thief"
106.	1/26	Drama:
		"The Shepherd of the Hills"
107.	2/11	Drama:
		"The Girl He Sent Away"
108.	2/13	Drama: Baptist Ladies Aid Society Benefit
		"Dot, the Miner's Daughter" (local talent)
109.	2/23	Drama: United Play Co., Inc.
		"Lavender and Old Lace"
110.	3/6	Drama: Jones and Crane, Inc.
		"The Virginian"
111.	5/1**	Drama: The Syndicate
		"The Broken Rosary"
112.	5/8	Concert: Schoolhouse sidewalk fund (local talent)

* This and the remaining Lyceum Course events may have been held in the newly built Lyric
Theatre.
** W. A. Eiler's New Orleans Minstrels on April 10 and the Mollie Bailey Circus on June 10
were under canvas.

113.	5/13	Drama: Albert Taylor Company "Lend Me Your Baby"
114.	After 7/2	Concert: Margaret Huff and Choir* "The Holy City"
115.	8/4	Banquet: Woodmen of the World
116.	11/12–11/14	Dramas: Gilson-Bradfield Stock Company 11/12: "Barriers Burned Away"

---

* M. A. Ware, "Forty Years of Music in the Lubbock Public Schools (1900–1940)," Texas Technological College Master's Thesis, 1941, p. 16.

Appendix C

KNOWN PERFORMANCES OF THE LUBBOCK BAND
AND THE LUBBOCK COWBOY BAND (Location given where known):

ENTRY #	DATE	EVENT

The Lubbock Band (N. C. Bishop, Director)

1912

1.	6/29	Firemen's benefit, Airdome
2.	7/26	Political rally, Bandstand
3.	8/2	Old Soldiers' Reunion, Gomez
4.	8/8	Evening concert, Bandstand
5.	10/11	Play: "Uncle Josh," Opera House
6.	10/24	Play: "Uncle Josh," Crosbyton
7.	11/15	Play: "The Face at the Window," Opera House

The Lubbock Cowboy Band (Monte Bowron, Director)

1913

8.	5/5	First Monday (of the month) Trades Day
9.	5/23	Concert, Bandstand
10.	5/?	Meeting to organize Lubbock Chamber of Commerce
11.	6/2	Trades Day
12.	6/19—	Weekly Thursday evening concerts, Bandstand
13.	6/26	Picnic celebrating railroad, Shallowater
14.	7/4	Formal opening of Littlefield
15.	7/7	Trades Day
16.	7/10	Delegation from Amarillo, Depot
17.	8/4	Trades Day
18.	8/8	Old Soldiers' Reunion, Brownfield
19.	8/8 & 8/9	Convention of Sunday School specialists
20.	9/1	Trades Day
21.	10/6	Lubbock County Fair (& Trades Day)
22.	11/3	Trades Day

1914

23.	2/15	Concert
24.	2/22	Concert
25.	4/5	Trades Day
26.	5/25	Intermission feature? Lyric Theatre
27.	6/9	Intermission feature? Lyric Theatre
28.	6/11	Colorado-Gulf Highway Delegation
29.	6/26—	Weekly Friday evening concerts, Bandstand
30.	7/4	Fourth of July picnic, Vaughn

1915

31.	7/4	Fourth of July celebration, Brownfield

1916

32.	9/13	Delegation from Abilene, Bandstand (?)

Endnotes

Chapter 1

1. Much of the above account was summarized from Seymour V. Connor, "The First Settlers" and "The Founding of Lubbock," in *A History of Lubbock*, Lawrence L. Graves, editor (Lubbock, Texas, 1962), pp. 45–97, and from Myra Ann Perkins, "Pioneer Lubbock, 1891–1909," Master's Thesis, Texas Technological College (1941), pp. 1–46.

2. Smylie C. Wilson, interview by Jean A. Paul, June 25, 1958, for the Southwest Collection, Texas Tech University, Lubbock, Texas, typescript, p. 10.

3. Willie Mae Hawthorne, "A Short History of Lubbock County," n.d., 24 pp., typescript copy in the Southwest Collection, Texas Tech University, p. 6.

4. W. O. Tubbs, "The Llano Estacado," n.d., 21 pp., typescript copy in the Southwest Collection, Texas Tech University, p. 6.

5. Connor, p. 86

6. George M. Hunt, *Early Days Upon the Plains of Texas* (Lubbock, Texas, 1919), p. 36. Also Seymour V. Connor, "The New Century," in *A History of Lubbock,* p. 107.

7. An undated clipping from *The Lubbock Avalanche–Journal* quoting Mrs. George C. Wolffarth (Lottie Hunt), Southwest Collection, Texas Tech University.

8. Perkins, p. 81, as related by Mrs. George C. Wolffarth in 1939.

9. "Memoirs of Maggie Lee Holden," n.d., about 250 loose pages, typescript copy in the Southwest Collection, Texas Tech University, p. 14.

10. Untitled document by Mrs. Horace Hartsell, n.d., 7 pp., typescript copy in the Southwest Collection, Texas Tech University, p. 7; and Wolffarth, undated clipping.

11. Perkins, pp. 81–82.

12. Connor, p. 89; *The Avalanche*, October 13, 1905, p. 2. The latter figure may have been overly optimistic.

13. *The Avalanche,* July 14, 1905, p. 3. Errors in spelling and typographical mistakes in the newspaper will be routinely corrected without notice throughout this work.

14. *Ibid.*, August 4, 1905, p. 2.

15. *Ibid.*, p. 3.

16. *Ibid.*, September 15, 1905, p. 4; October 6, 1905, p. 1.

17. *Ibid.*, October 20, 1905, p. 2 and October 27, 1905, p. 1.

18. *Ibid.*, December 8, 1905, p. 2.

19. *Ibid.*, August 11, 1905, p. 2; September 8, 1905, p.3.

20. *Ibid.*, December 22, 1905, pp. 1 and 3; January 5, 1906, p. 3.

21. *Ibid.*, December 22, 1905, p. 2.

Chapter 2

* Material from this Chapter is reprinted from the *Panhandle–Plains Historical Review,* Vol. LIX (1986), courtesy of the Panhandle–Plains Historical Society, Canyon, Texas.

1. Smylie C. Wilson, interview by Jean A. Paul, June 25, 1958, typescript, Southwest Collection, Texas Tech University, Lubbock, Texas, p. 10.

2. Mary Howell, *The Lubbock Avalanche–Journal,* July 26, 1959.

3. *Ibid.*

4. Wilson interview, p. 9.

5. "The Llano Estacado," typescript, n.d., Southwest Collection, Texas Tech University, p. 14.

6. Virginia Richmond Tubbs, interview by the author, May 2, 1975. Mrs. Tubbs was the daughter of S. A. Richmond and wife of W. Oscar Tubbs.

7. An article appearing in *The Avalanche,* November 29, 1907, p. 5, indicated a capacity of 450–500, but that figure may be too high.

8. Howell, *The Lubbock Avalanche–Journal,* July 26, 1959.

9. *The Avalanche,* November 29, 1907, p. 5.

10. Wilson interview, p. 7.

11. Ross Edwards, *Fiddle Dust* (Denver, 1965), p. 44.

12. Tubbs interview.

13. *The Avalanche,* August 2, 1907, p. 8; *ibid.,* August 16, 1907, p. 1; *ibid.,* September 27, 1907, p. 1.

14. *Ibid.,* April 10, 1908, p. 1.

15. *Ibid.,* December 6, 1907, p. 5; *ibid.,* December 13, 1907, p. 1; *ibid.,* January 17, 1908, p.8.

16. *Ibid.,* February 25, 1909, p. 1.

17. *Ibid.,* January 15, 1909, p. 1.

18. *Ibid.,* August 9, 1907, p. 5; *ibid.,* August 16, 1907, p. 8.

19. *Ibid.,* September 4, 1908, p. 5; *ibid.,* October 2, 1908, p. 5.

20. Seymour V. Connor, "The New Century," in *A History of Lubbock,* ed. Lawrence L. Graves (Lubbock, Texas, 1962), p. 119.

21. *Thirteenth Census of the United States,* Taken in 1910; *The Avalanche,* October 23, 1908, p. 1. The newspaper was renamed *The Lubbock Avalanche* in late April or early May 1909.

Chapter 3

1. Mickel, Jere C., *Footlights on the Prairie* (St. Cloud, Minnesota, 1974), p. 13.

2. Toll, Robert C., *On with the Show* (New York, 1976), p. 143.

3. Slout, William L., *Theatre in a Tent: The Development of a Provincial Entertainment* (Bowling Green, Ohio, 1972), p. 6.

4. Toll, p. 5.

5. *Ibid.,* p. 10.

6. *Ibid.,* pp. 147–48.

7. Mickel, pp. 6 and 23.

8. *The Lubbock Avalanche,* April 15, 1909, p. 2 and June 3, 1909, p. 4, respectively.

9. Mary Howell, *The Lubbock Avalanche–Journal,* July 26, 1959.

10. Contrary to the newspaper report (April 8, 1909, p. 1), "The building will [have] a fifteen-foot stage fifty feet wide," the stage could scarcely have been fifty feet wide, as the building itself was only either 30' or 40' wide. Since the October 3, 1912 issue reported that the theater was enlarged 150 square feet by moving the stage back five feet, the width of the stage (and the building as well) must have been 30' (30' X 5' = 150 square feet). Hence, the stage was most likely 15' deep and 30' wide.

11. *The Lubbock Avalanche,* May 13, 1909, p. 6.

12. Howell, *ibid.*

13. Erving McElroy interview to David Murrah, Texas Tech University Southwest Collection, June 1, 1972; *The Lubbock Avalanche,* October 3, 1912, p. 1.

14. *The Lubbock Avalanche,* May 20, 1909, p. 8.

15. *Ibid.*, September 16, 1909, Part II, p. 8.

16. *Record of Ordinances,* City of Lubbock, Vol. I:

Ordinance No. 3, Article 1 (April 16, 1909):

... on and after the day of the passage of this Ordinance, there shall be imposed upon all Public Exhibitions, Theatrical Performances, Dramatic Presentations, etc., a Tax of five dollars ($5.00) for each performance provided that nothing in this Ordinance shall be construed to apply to exhibitions for charitable purposes or to those given by home talent.

Ordinance No. 10, Article 2 (May 21, 1909):

It shall be unlawful for any person to give or to be concerned in giving or exhibiting any variety show, theater, concert, moving picture show, or any other kind of show within the corporate limits of Lubbock on Sunday.

Ordinance No. 11, Article 2 (May 21, 1909):

... for any moving picture exhibition where specialty acts or performers are used during intermission of pictures, the Tax shall be two dollars and fifty cents ($2.50) for each night's exhibition.

Ordinance No. 12, Article 1 (June 1, 1909):

... any person in charge of [a] show or Traveling Company or manager of same or one who is responsible for payment of all or any Taxes or licenses for same who fails to pay the license imposed in Ordinance 3, of the City of Lubbock, before the beginning of any performance or public exhibition, shall be guilty of [a] misdemeanor ...

17. *The Avalanche,* April 8, 1909, p. 1.

18. *The Lubbock Avalanche,* May 13, 1909, p. 4, and May 27, 1909, p. 1.

19. *Ibid.,* May 27, 1909, p. 1; June 3, p. 2; and July 8, p. 9.

20. *Ibid.,* February 17, 1910, p. 4.

21. *Ibid.,* May 20, 1909, p. 8.

22. *Ibid.,* September 2, 1909, p. 11 and November 11, 1909, p. 1.

23. *Ibid.,* May 13, 1909, p. 5; August 12, p. 6; November 11, p. 1; and June 2, 1910, p. 4.

24. Lawrence L. Graves, ed., *A History of Lubbock* (Lubbock, Texas, 1962), p. 225.

25. *The Lubbock Avalanche,* November 25, 1909, p. 15.

26. *Ibid.,* November 11, 1909, p. 1.

27. *Ibid.,* February 10, 1910, p. 14

28. *Ibid.,* November 25, 1909, p. 16.

29. The Albert Taylor Company came during the week of October 10, 1910, and again for three days during the week of March 27, 1911; also Maudena's Musical Comedy on November 23–24, 1910.

30. *The Lubbock Avalanche,* December 14, 1911.

31. Unavailable issues of the *Avalanche* from January to May most likely include other companies.

32. *Ibid.,* August 28, 1913, p. 12.

33. Later corrected to Dec. 8th.

34. *Ibid.,* September 25, 1913, p. 12 and October 9, 1913, p. 1.

35. *Ibid.,* October 23, 1913, p. 12 and October 30, 1913, p. 1.

36. *Ibid.,* March 7, 1912, p. 1.

37. *Ibid.,* May 2, 1912, p. 1 *et passim.*

38. *Ibid.,* May 23, 1912, p. 8.

39. *Ibid.,* October 10, 1912, p. 8 *et passim.*

40. *Ibid.,* October 3, 1912, p. 1.

41. Interview, Roy McElroy, June 23, 1987.

42. *The Lubbock Avalanche,* June 25, 1914, p. 1.

43. The advertising, however, was not entirely consistent.

44. *The Lubbock Avalanche,* August 28, 1913, p. 1. The impermanent airdome was closed down after the opening of the Lyric, whose large fans made it a suitable replacement for the open-air theater during the summertime.

45. The seeds for this second theater were sown after a disastrous fire of New Year's Eve 1913 that destroyed several wooden buildings on the west side of the courthouse square. When owner R. H. Lowrey rebuilt, McElroy seized the opportunity to lease a more solid building in a superior location.

46. *The Lubbock Avalanche,* October 16, 1913, p. 12.

Chapter 4

* Material from this Chapter is reprinted from the *West Texas Historical Association Yearbook,* Vol. LX (1984), courtesy of the West Texas Historical Association, Abilene, Texas.

1. Hazen, Margaret and Robert, *The Music Men: An Illustrated History of Brass Bands in America, 1800–1920* (Washington, D.C., 1987), p. xvii.

2. *Ibid.,* p. xviii *et passim.*

3. Fennell, Frederick, *Time and the Winds* (Kenosha, Wisconsin, 1954), pp. 37–39.

4. Rudolph Wurlitzer Company, *Catalog No. 122* (Chicago, Illinois, c. 1917), p. 7, as quoted in Hazen, p. 4.

5. Hazen, p. 4.

6. *Ibid.,* pp. 64–65.

7. Nomenclature for brass instruments, owing to the large variety of types and sizes and to many hybrids and other variables, is rather confusing; only the most common instruments, therefore, are listed here.

8. Hazen, p. 139.

9. Smylie C. Wilson Interview, typescript, Southwest Collection, Texas Tech University, pp. 7–8. See also *Lubbock Avalanche–Journal,* April 6, 1941, p. 19 and May 30, 1968, p. 1.

10. Wilson Interview, pp. 8–9. A check of the Conn Music Company revealed that all records prior to 1928 were destroyed by fire.

11. *Ibid.,* p. 11.

12. *Ibid.,* p. 10.

13. *Ibid.* Wilson also remembered playing at picnics and Fourth of July celebrations and in the bandstand that was built on the courthouse square, but that could not have involved the original band since the bandstand wasn't built until 1912 (*The Lubbock Avalanche,* July 4, 1912, p. 7).

14. There is confusion regarding authorship of the source, although the information itself is not in question. Tanner Laine and Frank Hayne both related this account with virtually identical wording, Laine in a booklet celebrating the seventy-fifth anniversary of Lubbock County ("Seems Only Yesterday," prepared for the American State Bank, without date [1966?] or pagination; a copy is in the Southwest Collection) and Hayne in his master's thesis on Clifford E. Hunt (Texas Technological College, 1948, pp. 48–50). However, Laine claimed his source to be a diary by Clifford Hunt ("Historical Diary of Lubbock County," n.d., no pagination, typescript, in the possession of the Hunt family; a copy is in the Southwest Collection), while Hayne credited a 1948 interview with Smylie Wilson.

Some light may be shed on the situation, for it is peculiar that Frank Hayne knew and used the Hunt diary for his thesis, but does not credit it as his source for the above account; moreover, if there ever was such information in the diary, it is no longer there. Mrs. Howard Hunt kindly permitted me to examine the original document; it (presently) contains no information about the Lubbock band. When apprised of this situation, Mr. Laine conceded to me that it is possible he got the story from some other source.

15. Issues of *The Avalanche* that doubtless would have recorded the birth of both bands are unavailable.

16. "The Lubbock 1906 Band will give a grand musical program on the night of the 29th (Thanksgiving). The program will consist of band selections, recitations, quartets and other features. Lubbock should turn out en masse and give the band boys a rousing reception. They are entitled to it and the funds will certainly go toward a pleasant and worthy cause." *The Lubbock Leader,* November 15, 1906, p. 3. Original issue was located in the Panhandle–Plains Historical Museum, Canyon, Texas; microfilm copy now in Southwest Collection.

17. Numerous copies of the Plate 3 photograph exist, including a greatly enlarged one hanging in the Lubbock Memorial Civic Center main gallery. I know of two copies of the photograph in Plate 4, one in the Texas Tech Museum (File No. 43–6–1) and one owned by Mr. Lawrence Green, son of one of the band members. There exists still another photograph of this band taken on July 4, 1907; the bandsmen are seated in the bandwagon during the parade, but are scarcely distinguishable (*Lubbock Avalanche–Journal,* July 26, 1959).

18. File No. 65–37–4 (c).

19. Both the list accompanying the photograph and the list given above (p. 35) for Lubbock's original band include a Mr. McDonald — the only person on the two lists with no first name or initials. If that circumstance were taken to suggest an older man, then a conflict would arise, for the man in the top row, second from right, identified as Mr. McDonald, looks like the youngest man in the band. It also seemed curious that Clifford Hunt was not in the photo, since he was in the original band, was living in Lubbock at the time, and was twenty years of age, about that of the man in the photograph. I asked Mrs. Howard Hunt, his daughter-in-law, and Mrs. L. Earl Hunt, his niece by marriage, if either could find Clifford in the photo. Each, independently, selected the man previously identified as Mr. McDonald. Clinching the identification is the indication in the list of the original band members that Hunt played a tenor horn, McDonald drum: In the photo, the man in question is indeed holding a tenor horn.

That answer raises another question, namely, why isn't Hunt listed in the "Souvenir Edition"? The only suggestion I can offer is that by September, Hunt was in the process of opening Lubbock's first dairy, about two and one-half miles south of town. Perhaps the workload of his new business or the distance from town forced him to drop out of the band by September.

20. First, given the very name of the band, the document cannot predate 1906, and the Staked Plains Telephone Company advertisement advances the year to 1907 (Figure 3). Yet the publication cannot be later than fall 1909, for "Facts About Lubbock" indicates that the railroad had not yet come (Figure 5). "Facts" also notes the presence of two newspapers in Lubbock, which would have been *The Avalanche* and *The Lubbock Leader.* Since the latter published only from November 15, 1906 to November 22, 1907, after which it was absorbed by its rival, "Souvenir Edition" must have been printed in 1907, and before November 22.

An earlier date than November 22, 1907, is indicated by the following: 1. *The Avalanche* on September 27 (p. 2) reported a population of 1,000 for Lubbock; "Facts" puts the number at about 900. 2. S. C. Turkenkopf, piccolo player in the "Souvenir Edition" list, moved to Amarillo in September or October, according to notices in *The Avalanche* in October and November. 3. The November 4 *Avalanche* contained advertisements for five physicians. The fifth was Dr. J. W. Overton who came to Lubbock in September 1907 to join the practice of his brother, Dr. M. C. Overton. "Facts" informs us that at the time the "Souvenir Edition" was published there were only four physicians in Lubbock. 4. The September 27 *Avalanche* (p. 3) reported that W. B. Leeman had left Lubbock on September 25 to take up residence in Colorado City; the October 11 issue (p. 8) confirmed his arrival in that city. It is certainly more likely that Mr. Leeman was a Lubbock resident rather than a resident of Colorado City at the time Lubbock honored him by circulating a souvenir edition of his composition "Eleanor Waltzes."

On the basis of those four points, a date much after the beginning of September 1907 would be out of the question. On the basis of two others, a date before August would be impossible: 1. According to *The Avalanche* (August 2, 1907, p. 5), Mr. Homer Kern took over as manager of the Nicolett Hotel on August 1; in the advertisement for the Nicolett Hotel, Kern is listed as manager (Figure 3). 2. Dr. M. C. Overton advertised in the August 2 *Avalanche* (p. 8) that his newly purchased Overton Addition will be divided into residential lots and soon put on the market. "If you want a home in Lubbock do not buy till this is ready." Yet the "Souvenir Edition" advertisement (Figure 4) indicates that the Overton Addition "is rapidly filling up with nice homes," suggesting a time at least a month later. Hence, a date around the first of September for the "Souvenir Edition" can be accepted with a fair degree of confidence.

21. *The Avalanche*, November 8, 1907, p. 1.

22. *Ibid.*, September 30, 1909, p. 7.

23. *Ibid.*, September 7, 1907, p. 2.

24. *Ibid.*, November 8, 1907, p. 1.

25. The article also noted: "The proceeds of this entertainment will be used by the band to defray the expenses of same. It takes money to keep up a first class band and recognizing the value a band is to a town the citizens should feel under obligations to support it, especially when they have never asked for a contribution since it was organized without giving value received in return." *The Avalanche*, October 18, 1907, p. 1.

26. *Ibid.*, October 25, 1907, p. 1.

27. ". . . the Lubbock Band is purely a public benefactor. It was organized for the purpose of helping to build up the town and every one is bound to admit that it has been the source of much favorable comment from visitors. The members of the organization have sacrificed their time and money to make the band what it is . . . but it is not right that they should have to go down into their pockets individually and put up money to defray the expense of hall rents, lights, advertising, etc . . . They have not a cent in the treasury at this time . . . They are at a monthly expense of $50 . . . for hall rent and instructor's fees, not mentioning the lighting and heating of the hall. It is plain, therefore, that to maintain the Lubbock band they must be at an expense of $60 to $70 per month." *The Avalanche*, November 8, 1907, p. 1.

28. It seems to me that in order to realize $70, they would have had to sell about 235 tickets; I am assuming an audience made up about equally of adults at thirty-five cents admission and children at twenty-five cents (ticket prices are given in the November 8 advertisement). Now 235 people would have been about twenty-five percent of the entire Lubbock population at that time (*The Avalanche*, September 27, 1907, p. 2, reported a population of 1,000).

29. *The Avalanche*, November 8, 1907, p. 8.

30. "The Lubbock Band, last evening at their hall, rendered an excellent program, consisting of music, overtures and special selections on the piano by three ladies. The entertainment concluded with several acts in up-to-date negro dress, style, and dialect." *The Avalanche*, November 15, 1907, p. 8.

31. S. J. Winn, president, Z. D. Agnew, vice-president, W. B. Powell, secretary/treasurer, S. C. Wilson, director, and W. A. Custis and E. B. Green, custodians.

32. The February 14, 1908, *Avalanche* (p. 8) notice of a concert on February 17 is both brief and startling: "The Lubbock Band will give a free concert in their hall next Monday night. Plenty of good music will be rendered by the band on this occasion absolutely free. Come out and enjoy yourselves for an hour or so." No clue was given why this concert was free, but I suspect this and the next concert were originally planned as one. Too much material resulted in a split into two performances five days apart. Admission was charged only for the second.

The last recorded activity of this band, on February 22, received the following notice: "The Lubbock Band enjoyed quite a liberal patronage in their entertainment Saturday night, at which time they presented 'Tony the Convict.' The receipts from this play were about $80.00" (*The Avalanche*, February 28, 1908, p. 7).

33. *Ibid.*, January 24, 1908, p. 3.

34. These were not large orchestras, merely groups of five to ten players including strings, brass, and piano.

35. *The Avalanche*, August 9, 1907, p. 5.

36. *Ibid.*, August 26, 1909, p. 14.

37. W. B. Leeman and S. C. Turkenkopf left Lubbock around the end of September (see p. 105); C. H. Lister left in January (*The Avalanche*, January 3, 1908, p. 5); and in February Will Crawford was in Illinois taking a course in watch adjustment (*The Avalanche*, February 28, 1908, p. 5). All four were experienced players.

38. The July 31 *Avalanche* (p. 5) reported that Mr. Carlock had gone to Paduach to "take charge of the band at that place. Mr. Carlock is a young man of great musical talent and has rendered good service to the Lubbock Band during his stay with us." The August 14 paper (p. 8) referred to him as "the band teacher." The November 8 article mentioned that the band was paying an instructor (Note 27); in all probability, it was Ed Carlock.

39. H. B. Earnest, S. J. Winn, W. B. Powell, H. R. Mason, S. C. Wilson, W. M. Ross, and Z. D. Agnew (*The Avalanche*, December 23, 1909, p. 9).

40. The band's $123.40 earnings from the Christmas time production in 1907 could scarcely have derived from an audience of less than 400, about forty percent of the population.

Chapter 5

1. *The Lubbock Avalanche*, December 23, 1909, p. 9; May 12, 1910, p. 15.

2. *Ibid.*, June 22, 1911.

3. *Ibid.*, July 6, 1911, p. 1.

4. *Ibid.*, March 28, 1912, p. 1.

5. *Ibid.*, September 21, 1911, p. 2.

6. *Ibid.*, February 8, 1912, p. 6.

7. *Ibid.*, May 9, 1912, p. 14.

8. *Ibid.*, June 13, 1912, p. 1.

9. *Ibid.*, July 4, 1912, p. 1.

10. *Ibid.*, p. 7.

11. See Chapter 4.

12. *The Lubbock Avalanche*, October 24, 1912, p. 8 and November 7, 1912, p. 7.

13. *Ibid.*, May 22, 1913, p. 1.

14. *Ibid.*, June 26, 1913, p. 7.

15. *Ibid.*, May 8, 1913, pp. 1 and 6. Admirers of George Hunt will note that this poem constitutes an addition to the poems printed in his *Early Days Upon the Plains of Texas* (1919).

16. *Ibid.*, May 22, 1913, p. 1 and also May 15, 1913, p. 9.

17. *Ibid.*, May 22, 1913, p. 1.

18. *Ibid.*, February 26, 1914, Section II, p. 1.

19. *Ibid.*, May 29, 1913, p. 3.

20. *Ibid.*, p. 12.

21. *Ibid.*, August 14, 1913, p. 9.

22. *Ibid.*, June 12, 1913, p. 9.

23. *Ibid.*, July 3, 1913, p. 10.

24. David Gracy, II, *Littlefield Lands: Colonization on the Texas South Plains, 1912–1920*, University of Texas Press, copyright 1968, pp. 9–31. Also *Lubbock Ava-*

lanche–Journal, article by Nilah Rodgers, July 4, 1975, p. 87; *Lamb County Leader*, Littlefield, Texas, June 27, 1963, p. 8; and *The Lubbock Avalanche*, June 26, 1913, p. 1.

25. Though Bowron had taken the position prior to the establishment of The Lubbock Chamber of Commerce, he undoubtedly made a financial arrangement with the businessmen of town, as did his predecessor N. C. Bishop. See above, p. 53.

26. *The Lubbock Avalanche*, May 28, 1914, Section II, p. 12.

27. *Ibid.*, p. 12.

28. A few issues can be found in the Southwest Collection, Texas Tech University, and at The Barker Texas History Center, The University of Texas at Austin.

29. File # 0074–44–0098.

30. Wood markings — light and dark shaded boards around the two doorways — are identical.

31. Southwest Collection, Photographic Collection (SWCPC) 57 (i) E7.

32. There is another photograph, not presented here, given to the author by Mr. Condie Caraway about ten years ago, that shows fifteen bandsmen in uniform but without instruments. They match exactly the fifteen in Plate 6.

33. Interviews conducted during August 1986.

34. Dolly Bowron and *Lubbock Avalanche–Journal*, March 4, 1956 and January 6, 1952.

35. Chamber records do indicate payment of a salary to the band director of The Lubbock Chamber of Commerce Band, 1919–1922. Evidence presented above suggests a similar arrangement for the Lubbock Cowboy Band.

36. Interview conducted January 13, 1981.

37. Annielee Clark quickly identified her uncle Alva M. Rankin as the bandsman holding the helicon, thus confirming Rev. Partin's identification.

38. Wilson, by his daughter Frances; Ross, by his brother-in-law Condie Caraway (Interview, July 1975).

39. "Economic, Social, and Cultural Developments," *A History of Lubbock* (Lubbock, Texas, 1962), pp. 219–220.

40. Interview, June 4, 1987.

41. Interview, June 13, 1987.

42. *The Lubbock Avalanche*, September 14, 1916, p. 1.

Chapter 6

1. M. A. Ware, "Forty Years of Music in the Lubbock Public Schools (1900–1940)," Master's Thesis, Texas Technological College, 1941, pp. 14–15.

2. *The Avalanche*, October 4, 1907, p. 1.

3. *Ibid.*, August 14, 1908, p. 5.

4. *The Lubbock Avalanche*, April 28, 1910, p. 4.

5. *Ibid.*, September 1, 1910, p. 3 and September 8, 1910, p. 2.

6. Mrs. William Claxton, Mrs. Carl Roberds, Mrs. Van Sanders, Mrs. Frank Wheelock, Mrs. W. O. Tubbs, Mrs. N. M. Akerson, Smylie Wilson, Willie Wilson, and Bonnie Hudgins.

7. *The Avalanche*, August 9, 1907, p. 1.

8. *Ibid.*, August 30, 1907, p. 5.

9. *Ibid.*, February 7, 1908, p. 1.

10. *The Lubbock Avalanche*, August 26, 1909, p. 14.

11. *Ibid.*, July 14, 1910 and October 27, 1910.

12. *The Avalanche*, December 8, 1905, p. 2. Admission was twenty-five cents, and since $36.00 was taken in, 144 people — almost twenty percent of the entire population — attended.

13. *Ibid.*, October 13, 1905, p. 2.

14. *Ibid.*, April 17, 1908, p. 1; June 10, 1909, p. 4; June 30, 1910.

15. *The Lubbock Avalanche*, June 23, 1910, p. 6; also June 30, 1910, p. 4.

16. *Ibid.,* May 26, 1910, p. 1.

17. *Ibid.,* August 25, 1910.

18. *Ibid.,* August 29, 1912, p. 7.

19. *Ibid.,* October 23, 1913, p. 12.

20. *Ibid.,* September 9, 1909, p. 1.

21. *Ibid.,* May 26, 1910, p. 1.

22. *Ibid.,* October 19, 1911, p. 10.

23. *Ibid.,* July 18, 1912, p. 8.

24. *Ibid.,* August 18, 1910.

25. November 19, 1910; February 10, 1911; and June 5, 1911.

26. *The Lubbock Avalanche,* June 15, 1911.

27. September 29, 1911; March 29, 1912; May 10, 1912.

28. *The Lubbock Avalanche,* August 29, 1912, p. 1.

29. *Ibid.,* November 21, 1912, p. 1.

30. *Ibid.,* October 23, 1919, p. 1.

31. Ware, pp. 15–16. Also *Lubbock Avalanche–Journal,* July 26, 1959.

32. *The Lubbock Avalanche,* August 25, 1910; also, several interviews in September 1987 with her niece Mrs. Dona Cavaness.

33. *Ibid.,* August 8, 1912, p. 8.

34. *Ibid.,* p. 10.

35. *Ibid.,* May 21, 1914, Section II, p. 11.

36. *Ibid.,* November 20, 1913, p. 14.

37. Ware, p. 17.

38. *The Lubbock Avalanche,* July 24, 1919, p. 5; also the Cavaness interviews.

39. *Ibid.,* December 23, 1921, p. 12 and July 7, 1922, p. 12.

40. Interviews conducted by the author with Cecile Meskimen, a fellow music teacher, on September 10, 1987; student Madge Webster on September 12, 1987; student Ruth Douglas on September 13, 1987; and fellow music teacher Mamie Neal on September 13, 1987.

41. *The Lubbock Avalanche,* June 5, 1913, p. 12.

42. *Ibid.,* July 10, 1913, p. 12.

43. *Ibid.,* September 14, 1916, p. 1.

44. *Ibid.,* October 2, 1913, p. 1.

45. *Ibid.,* May 14, 1914, p. 12.

46. *Ibid.,* November 14, 1918.

47. *Ibid.,* August 28, 1919, p. 10.

48. *Ibid.,* September 26, 1918, p. 1 and August 28, 1919, p. 1.

49. Paul Cutter, "A Triumph of Music Education: The Lubbock Public School System During the 1920's," forthcoming.

50. Taken from *The Avalanche,* February 7, 1908, p. 1; *The Lubbock Avalanche,* May 8, 1919, p. 24. (Mistakes not corrected).

51. *Ibid.,* October 16, 1913, p. 1; also October 9, 1913, p. 7.

52. *Ibid.,* May 14, 1914, p. 1.

53. *Ibid.,* p. 12.

54. *The Avalanche,* January 24, 1908, p. 3.

55. *Ibid.,* April 10, 1908, p. 1.

56. *The Lubbock Avalanche,* November 21, 1912, p. 1, and November 20, 1913, p. 4.

57. *The Avalanche,* February 7, 1908, p. 1.

58. *Ibid.,* July 24, 1908, p. 8.

59. *Ibid.,* July 31, 1908, p. 5, and September 4, 1908, p. 1.

60. *Ibid.,* August 21, 1908, p. 3. First names cannot be determined with certainty except for Lula Campbell and Mamie Neal.

61. *The Lubbock Avalanche,* April 28, 1910, p. 14.

62. *Ibid.,* February 17, 1910, p. 4 and February 3, 1910, p. 13.

63. *Ibid.,* July 14, 1910, p. 6 and October 27, 1910, p. 4.

64. *Ibid.,* August 29, 1912, p. 7.

65. *Ibid.,* October 17, 1912, p. 7 and December 26, 1912, p. 6.

66. *Ibid.,* June 19, 1913, p. 8.

67. *The Avalanche,* February 7, 1908, p. 1.

68. *The Lubbock Avalanche,* May 26, 1910, p. 1. Most of the information in this chapter regarding music in the Lubbock public school system was taken from *The Lubbock Avalanche.* Despite considerable effort and a gracious willingness to assist, Miss Frances Wilson of the Lubbock Independent School District's central offices was unable to locate any documents pertaining to music prior to 1925.

69. *Ibid.,* August 29, 1912, p. 1.

70. *Ibid.,* November 6, 1919, p. 1.

71. *Ibid.,* August 28, 1919, pp. 10 and 1.

72. *Ibid.,* May 13, 1920, p. 4.

73. *The Westerner* of 1918 includes a photograph of a 13-piece orchestra.

74. Ware, pp. 20–24.

75. 1917–18 information taken from Lubbock High School's *The Westerner,* 1918.

A Selected Bibliography

Apel, Willi. *Harvard Dictionary of Music,* 2nd Edition. Cambridge, Massachusetts, Harvard University Press, 1969.

The Avalanche. Lubbock, Texas, 1900–1909. Issues (incomplete) in the Southwest Collection, Texas Tech University.

Bronwell, Nancy B. *Lubbock: A Pictorial History.* The Donning Company, Virginia Beach, 1980.

Connor, Seymour V. ed., *Builders of the Southwest.* Lubbock, Texas, 1959.

Edwards, Ross. *Fiddle Dust.* Denver, Big Mountain Press, 1965.

Fennell, Frederick. *Time and the Winds.* Kenosha, Wisconsin, G. Leblanc Company, 1954.

Graves, Lawrence L. "Lubbock, Texas, History Collection: Material Gathered for *A History of Lubbock* (1962)," Typescript, n.d., the Southwest Collection, Texas Tech University.

Graves, Lawrence L. ed., *A History of Lubbock.* Lubbock, Texas, West Texas Museum Association, 1962.

Griggs, William C. ed., *A Pictorial History of Lubbock, Texas, 1880–1950.* Lubbock County Historical Commission, Lubbock, Texas, 1976.

Hartsell, Mrs. Horace. Untitled Article, Typescript, n.d., 7 pp., copy in the Southwest Collection, Texas Tech University.

Hawthorne, Willie Mae. "A Short History of Lubbock County," Typescript, n.d., 24 pp., copy in the Southwest Collection, Texas Tech University.

Hazen, Margaret and Robert. *The Music Men: An Illustrated History of Brass Bands in America.* Washington, D.C., Smithsonian Institution Press, 1987.

Hedges, R. Alan. "Actors Under Canvas: A Study of the Theatre of the Circuit Chautauqua, 1910–1933." Ph.D. Dissertation, The Ohio State University, 1976.

Holden, Maggie Lee. "Memoirs of Maggie Lee Holden," Typescript, n.d., about 250 loose pages, copy in the Southwest Collection, Texas Tech University.

Hunt, George M. *Early Days Upon the Plains of Texas.* Lubbock, Texas, Avalanche Printing Co., 1919.

Leeman, William B. "The Eleanor Waltzes," Promotional Brochure. Lubbock, Texas, 1907. Copy in the Southwest Collection, Texas Tech University.

Lowrey, E. J. "The Story of Lubbock," Typescript, n.d., 33 pp., copy in the Southwest Collection, Texas Tech University.

The Lubbock Avalanche. Lubbock, Texas, 1909–1923, available to the author from three sources: Southwest Collection, Texas Tech University, 1909–1911 plus scattered issues subsequently; Microfilm edition, Comgraphix, Southwest Microfilm Division, El Paso, Texas, 1908–1923; and Microfilm edition, The Barker Texas History Center, The University of Texas at Austin (original papers in The Barker Texas History Center), May 8–July 3, 1913 plus scattered issues subsequently.

Lubbock Avalanche–Journal. Lubbock, Texas, July 26, 1959.

Lubbock Chamber of Commerce. Minutes of Directors Meetings. Chamber of Commerce Office, Lubbock, Texas.

Lubbock, City Council Minutes. 1909–1917. City Secretary's Office, Lubbock, Texas.

Lubbock (City). Record of Ordinances. City Secretary's Office, Lubbock, Texas.

Lubbock County. Deed Records. County Courthouse, Lubbock, Texas.

The Lubbock Leader. Lubbock, Texas, November 15, 1906–November 22, 1907.

Mickel, Jere C. *Footlights on the Prairie.* St. Cloud, Minnesota, North Star Press, 1974.

Nye, Russel. *The Unembarrassed Muse: The Popular Arts in America.* New York, The Dial Press, 1970.

Perkins, Myra Ann. "Pioneer Lubbock, 1891–1909," Master's Thesis, Texas Technological College, 1941.

Rush, George P. "The Formative Years of Lubbock, Texas, 1909–1917," Master's Thesis, Texas Technological College, 1934.

Slout, William L. *Theatre in a Tent: The Development of a Provincial Entertainment.* Bowling Green, Ohio, Bowling Green University Popular Press, 1972.

Toll, Robert C. *On with the Show.* New York, Oxford University Press, 1976.

Tubbs, W. Oscar. "The Llano Estacado," Typescript, n.d., 21 pp., copy in the Southwest Collection, Texas Tech University.

Ware, Mary Anne. "Forty Years of Music in the Lubbock Public Schools (1900–1940)," Master's Thesis, Texas Technological College, 1941.

Wolffarth, Mrs. G. C. Undated *Lubbock Avalanche–Journal* newspaper clipping, the Southwest Collection, Texas Tech University.

Index